The Psychology of Discipline

Edited by

Darwin Dorr
Melvin Zax
Jack W. Bonner, III

INTERNATIONAL UNIVERSITIES PRESS, INC.

Madison   Connecticut

Library of Congress Cataloging in Publication Data
Main entry under title:

The Psychology of discipline.

Bibliography: p.
Includes Index
1. Discipline of children — Psychological
aspects. I. Dorr, Darwin, 1940-   .
II. Zax, Melvin, 1928-   . III. Bonner, Jack W., 1940-   .
BF723.D54P79   649'.64   81-20775
ISBN 0-8236-5581-4

Second Printing, 1986

Manufactured in the United States of America

To all children,
  our natural resource
  for the future

Contents

Acknowledgments

A large number of persons were very helpful in the production of this volume. Without question the most important person was Mrs. Bertie Phillips, secretary to Dr. Dorr. Mrs. Phillips typed countless letters as well as many, many drafts of each chapter. Additionally, she proofread nearly the entire manuscript, and saw to the many small and large details necessary for the completion of this project. We would also like to thank Mr. Tom Muncy, Ms. Deirdre Wiggins, and Mrs. Patricia Wyatt for helping us arrange the conference that was associated with the production of this book. Additionally, Mr. Robert Pozner and Mr. William Klodt, Research Technicians, and Mrs. Elizabeth Emily, Highland Hospital Librarian, were extremely helpful in aspects of literature searches. Finally, we would like to thank Mr. Patrick Covington for his critical editorial review of the manuscript.

The Editors

DARWIN DORR received his Ph.D. in Clinical Psychology from Florida State University. Originally trained in school psychology, he functioned as a school psychologist for nineteen schools prior to returning for doctoral training. His clinical internship at the University of Minnesota Hospital focused on children and youth. He has done research in the areas of prevention of emotional disorders in children, selection and training of paraprofessional workers, modeling and moral development, correlates of self-esteem, and behavior modification. He has held faculty positions at the University of Rochester, Washington University, and Duke University. Currently he is Chief Psychologist at Highland Hospital, Asheville, North Carolina.

MELVIN ZAX received his Ph.D. in Clinical Psychology from the University of Tennessee. Dr. Zax is Professor of Psychology at the University of Rochester, where he has spent most of his career, functioning for a period as Director of the Clinical Psychology Training Program. His diverse interests in psychology are reflected by the multiplicity of his publications. He has authored many fundamental textbooks in the area of clinical and community psychology.

JACK W. BONNER III was granted his M.D. degree from the University of Texas Southwestern Medical School. He interned at the University of Arkansas Medical Center and did his residency in psychiatry at Duke University. He is a board-certified psychiatrist. His current research and scholarly interests include the treatment of behaviorally disordered adolescents and the development of programs for psychiatrically disabled physicians. He has held the position of Assistant Professor, Duke University Medical Center. At present he is Medical Director, Highland Hospital, Asheville, North Carolina.

The Contributors

LORETTA K. CASS received her Ph.D. from Ohio State where she was a student of McCandless and Rotter. A mature clinician, she has published in the area of parent-child relationships. She held the rank of Associate Professor of Psychology and Medical Psychology at Washington University and she was the Chief Psychologist at Washington University Child Guidance Clinic for several years. She is now in retirement and active in the American Psychological Association.

MICHAEL CHANDLER received his Ph.D. from the University of California at Berkeley and did postdoctoral training at the Institut des Sciences de l'Éducation, Université des Genève in Switzerland and at the Menninger Foundation. At present he is with the Psychology Department, University of British Columbia, Vancouver, Canada. He has published extensively in clinical and developmental psychology.

VIRGINIA WATERS received her Ph.D. in School Psychology from Columbia University Teachers College. She has received honors in psychology as well as mathematics. She has several years' experience working with both normal and emotionally disturbed children. She served a two-year postdoctoral fellowship at the Institute for Advanced Study in Rational Psychotherapy and is currently Director of Children's Services at the Institute.

JAMES G. ALLEN is Professor of Psychiatry and Behavioral Sciences at the University of Oklahoma Medical Center. He received his M.D. from the University of Toronto and has trained in psychiatry and child psychiatry at McGill University, Baylor Medical School, and Harvard Medical School. He is a Fellow in the Royal College of Physicians and Surgeons of Canada. Although trained in psychoanalysis, he has been interested in transactional analysis in recent years and has done considerable work and teaching in this area.

BARBARA A. ALLEN is Clinical Associate Professor of Psychiatry, Tulsa Medical College and Visiting Professor of Human Relations, Department of Human Relations, University of Oklahoma. Dr. Allen holds the M.S.W. as well as the A.C.S.W. Additionally she has been awarded an M.P.H. in Human Ecology and a Ph.D. in Human Ecology from the University of Oklahoma. Her experience includes being a public school teacher, a hospital admissions officer, a family case worker, a deputy probation officer, a Y.W.C.A. and Job Corp counselor, a social worker, a clinical instructor in Psychiatric Social Work, and the private practice of social work.

ARTHUR ORGEL was awarded a Ph.D. by Florida State University and is presently Professor of Psychiatry, Pediatrics and Psychology, University of Rochester School of Medicine and Dentistry, where he is also Director of the Child Psychology Training Program. Dr. Orgel has had extensive experience in child clinical psychology and more specifically in psychotherapy with children. He has published in both experimental and clinical psychology and recently was a coauthor of a general psychology text.

CHARLES MADSEN, JR., is Professor of Psychology at Florida State University, teaching within the School Psychology Training Program. He received his Ph.D. from the University of Illinois and received early recognition in the field of behavior modification for his work on the elements of classroom control. He and his brother published *Parents, Children, Discipline: A Positive Approach,* which is a text manual based on the principles of behavioral modification.

JANE STEPHENS received her Ph.D. in School Psychology from Florida State University. She is a student and colleague of Charles Madsen and has done research on procedures for training parents in the use of behavior modification with their children. Presently she is Director of Pupil Personnel Services for the Buncombe County School District, North Carolina.

1

Introduction:
The Need to Understand Discipline

Darwin Dorr, Ph.D.

One may cite three major objectives of discipline. The first is to protect the child against external dangers and the results of childish impulsiveness. The second is to promote psychological development. Some degree of order and routine is necessary for a child to acquire the skills necessary for academic achievement and success in the work world. Children learn frustration tolerance by learning to moderate their desires, and they develop conscience by dealing with the consequences of their actions. Empathy, or consideration of basic human needs, is taught through discipline. Third, discipline encourages efficient group functioning. Limits must often be set on group activities to promote orderly, on-task behavior.[1]

Such a perspective on discipline argues that its purpose is not merely to make children "behave." Rather, discipline is a positive and significant concept in child development that is worthy of sustained professional attention. Why, then, has the subject received comparatively

[1] I am indebted to Drs. Linda Greensfelder and William Barley for their observations on this matter.

1

little such attention in modern psychology? The reason becomes clear when one realizes that contemporary beliefs regarding what constitutes proper discipline are strongly influenced by prevailing social and moral philosophies regarding children. As philosophy changes, so do views of discipline. During the Puritan Reformation the influential priest-educator Comenius cried: "I cannot refrain from severely reprimanding the shallow-brained mockery of affection in certain parents, who, conniving at everything, permit their children to grow up altogether without correction or discipline" (1653). Had modern psychology been in existence during the seventeenth century, one might whimsically speculate that there would have been much attention to the concept of discipline.

The birth date of modern psychology is traditionally said to be 1879, the date of the establishment of Wundt's laboratory in Leipzig. This date coincides almost exactly with the beginnings of major social reform movements in America (Levine and Levine, 1970). Shocked by the toxic by-products of social Darwinism, intellectuals, journalists, and reform-minded philosophers publicized the wretched plight of overworked, stunted, deprived, neglected children. The resulting outrage led to reforms which purged the factories of the child labor force. During the period of 1890–1910, there was an outpouring of concern for children's welfare which was expressed in the founding of the Family Services Association (1911), U.S. Children's Bureau (1912), National Federation of Settlements (1911), Boy Scouts of America (1910), Campfire Girls (1910), Girl Scouts (1912), Pathfinders of America (1914), and juvenile courts (1906). During this period, the visiting teacher, the visiting nurse, and the settlement house movement also emerged. Into this climate of social enlightenment and concern for children came science. Impressed by remarkable advances in chemistry and physics, Americans became fascinated with the idea that scientific method could be used to solve nearly any problem. Not surprisingly, those persons interested in children sought scientific information regarding ways to deal with vexing problems of child management. As a result of these forces, discipline based solely on parental authority gradually gave way to a more rational approach. In the twenties and thirties, proper child rearing tended to become more a matter of cleanliness, order, and routine. Habits strictly ordered from the first hour of life would be firmly established and endure, thus assuring a well-disciplined life.

In the thirties, however, the emergence of the teachings of psychoanalysis sensitized mental health workers to the role of frustration in the development of emotional problems. As a result, many began to question the desirability of overly regimented child-rearing patterns. By the forties and fifties, the belief was generally accepted that ideal child rearing should be organized around a strategy of unlimited tolerance of the child's need for gratification and a relatively limited emphasis on preparing the child to face the realities of the external world. To understand this development, it is helpful to remind ourselves that by the end of World War II, America was the most powerful and affluent nation in history. The majority of its people lived well. Social disruption was minimal, and the need to prepare a child to face the demands of a harsh, unyielding world seemed less urgent than in previous decades. It was a safe time to grow up. Hence, the time was right for the spirit of permissiveness. The exact meaning of permissiveness has probably been clouded and twisted beyond recognition. However, it is generally (and probably erroneously) accepted that permissiveness is the antithesis of discipline. For example, in 1960, A. S. Neill, creator of the ultrapermissive Summerhill School, declared: "A loving environment, without parental discipline, will take care of most of the troubles of childhood."

While it would be unreasonable to conclude that permissive child-rearing strategies were accepted by all quarters of society, it is clear that the concept of discipline was not in favor in health circles for many years.

Inevitably, however, the social climate changed. In the late sixties, our country's stability was shaken by Vietnam. Infinite American optimism slowly began to give way to the recognition that our society was not infallible — that our wealth and power were not unlimited and that a prosperous, comfortable future was not guaranteed. These factors may have contributed to a rekindling of interest in self-moderation and in the development of personal competencies, subjects relevant to the psychology of discipline. In 1970, James Dobson published *Dare to Discipline*, a popular book that sold over a million copies. In 1974, Dr. Benjamin Spock, often criticized for promoting ultrapermissive child-rearing patterns, labeled himself "antipermissive." In 1979, historian Christopher Lasch characterized America as a narcissistic, morally bankrupt society in which there is little real concern for future generations. Lasch argued that the course of precipitous decline might be reversed by reembracing the spirit of self-discipline:

> The moral discipline formerly associated with the work ethic retains a value independent of the role it once played in the defense of property rights. That discipline — indispensable to the task of building a new order — endures most of all in those who knew the old order only as a broken promise, yet who took the promise more seriously than those who merely took it for granted. [1979, pp. 235–236]

It is safe to say that there is a greater sympathy today for the concept of discipline than in the previous several decades. The time is right to intensify a study of discipline. Social sanction, however, is not necessarily a proper reason to embark on a study of psychological phenomena. There are more compelling reasons to examine the topic.

While the attainment of a substantial degree of self-discipline is a reasonable goal, the process of acquiring this discipline is often difficult. Patterns of self-discipline are established as the youngster is compelled to reconcile infantile impulses with environmental demands and restrictions. This interface, often stormy for child and adult, is an ongoing crisis. If it is consistently mismanaged, the youngster may become inhibited and overly controlled or impulsive and unsocialized. Ideally, however, this interface will be managed in ways that allow our children to grow to be adults who have learned how to satisfy their own needs while respecting the rights of others. Discipline is a serious and difficult challenge. Though rarely addressed in the professional literature, clinical experience reveals that discipline is a major concern of parents, teachers, and others who directly care for children. There is thus a need for more professional attention to the subject.

Another reason to focus on discipline is provided by recent studies showing that child abuse is epidemic in this country (Bakan, 1971; Gil, 1970). These studies resulted in a growing awareness of the problem of child abuse followed naturally by vigorous attempts to identify child abusers and to protect children (Child Abuse Prevention Act, 1973; Kempe and Helfer, 1972).

Child abuse is not an extreme application of discipline, but rather, a total breakdown in the disciplinary process. Most studies (see Spinetta and Rigler, 1972) have found that child abusers are typically ineffective disciplinarians. Their children are apt to be totally out of control and to be attacked savagely in retaliation. Some experts on child abuse feel that everyone who deals with children is a potential child abuser. For these reasons, we[2] feel that it is unwise to ignore the topic of discipline. Rather, it is mandatory that we focus on discipline in an attempt to develop and understand effective and humane ways to teach our children self-control and moral character, which, in turn, may help discourage child abuse.

It would be an error to conclude that we know nothing of the subject of discipline. The substantial body of theory and research on child development contains much information that is directly and indirectly relevant. For example, empirical studies have found several undesired outcomes of overly permissive, overly harsh, and inconsistent discipline. There is evidence that children of overly permissive and overly indulgent parents may develop into spoiled, selfish, inconsiderate, and demanding adults (Becker, 1964; Pollack, 1968). High permissiveness and low punishment in the home have been found to correlate positively with antisocial and aggressive behavior, particularly during middle and late childhood (Sears, 1961). On the other hand, overly severe, harsh, and restrictive child-rearing methods have also been associated with harmful effects (Becker, 1964). Such repressiveness may be associated with rebelliousness and socially deviant behavior, poor initiative and responsibility, low self-esteem, and the development of fear and hatred of the punishing person (Winder and Rau, 1962). These youngsters may also develop into overconforming adults who do not have the emotional strength to satisfy their own needs or to have a positive effect on their environment. Inconsistent discipline, harsh one time and lenient the next, has been associated with aggressive behavior (Deur

[2] While Chapters 1 and 8 were prepared by Dr. Dorr, the book *in toto* was a collaborative effort. Thus, the first person plural is often used.

and Parke, 1970; McCord, McCord, and Zola, 1959; Rosenthal, 1962; Sears, Maccoby, and Levin, 1957).

Interestingly, a study by Schvaneveldt, Freyer, and Ostler (1970), who interviewed preschool children regarding their perception of "good fathers" and "bad fathers," found that, among other things, "good fathers" do not spank you, but "bad fathers" let their children be naughty. Coopersmith (1968) reported that parents of high self-esteem children prove to be less permissive than those of children with low self-esteem. Further, the World Health Organization (1962), in a study on mental health in children, indicated that there is a growing tendency to recognize that modest discipline coupled with love is a more productive and helpful approach to raising children than is either extreme permissiveness or extreme punitiveness.

One of the most thorough studies of child-management patterns is that directed by Baumrind (1966, 1967, 1968, 1971a, 1971b, 1975). Provoked by the arguments for extreme permissiveness in the forties and fifties, Baumrind began a major research program on the effect of child-rearing approaches on the development of competence in children. Baumrind distinguished among "permissive," "authoritarian," and "authoritative" parenting. An authoritative parent is described as one who attempts to direct the child's activities in a rational, issue-oriented manner. The parent exerts firm control when parent and child differ but does not inhibit the child with unnecessarily strict controls. The authoritative parent asserts his or her rights but also respects the rights of the child. Reason and parental power are used to achieve child-rearing objectives. The authoritative parent is not easily swayed by the child's desires or by social pressure yet is not deluded by feelings of personal infallibility. Based on her extensive research, Baumrind concluded that authoritative

parents are more likely to facilitate the development of
competence in the form of responsible and independent
behavior than authoritarian or permissive parents.

Both the social climate and recent research support
the belief that discipline is a positive concept of considerable importance to the process of child development. But
how do we go about the work of discipline? There are
many theoretical points of view regarding how one should
deal with children. Proponents regarding various points
of view often differ in practical as well as theoretical
ways. Discrepancies in point of view prevail in professional and popular literature, which, in turn, may con-
fuse and frustrate conscientious students of child management.

When confronted with the array of seemingly dis-
crepant points of view, it is tempting to adopt one theory
and exclude others. Yet, we are committed to the belief
that in most cases integration and *rapprochement* are
preferable to orthodoxy in attempting to understand
ways to deal with human problems. Guided by our conceptualization of these issues, we decided to proceed in a
way that differs slightly from the norm. Most typically,
investigators develop a theory or model which is then
tested in application to an array of problems. We chose
to focus our attention on one problem, discipline, and to
examine ways in which several major theories may contribute to our understanding of and attempts to deal with
the problem.

This book provides the reader with a review of several points of view regarding approaches to discipline for
children and youth. The number of potentially helpful
theories is very large, and pragmatism required that we
limit ourselves to six. The approaches selected were psychoanalysis, Piagetian and other cognitive psychologies,
rational-emotive therapy, transactional analysis, the

views of Haim Ginott, and behavioral approaches. Freudian psychoanalysis was chosen because of its richness and pervasive influence on modern life. As a central theory of personality, psychoanalysis must either be accepted or rejected. It cannot be ignored. Piaget wrote virtually nothing on the subject of discipline. However, Piaget's brilliant conceptualizations of cognitive development and the related researches on morality were suspected to be a rich reservoir of information that would clarify aspects of the psychology of discipline. Rational-Emotive Therapy (RET) represents a studied departure from classical psychoanalysis. The direct, no-nonsense, cognitive approach advocated by RET promised to offer an interesting alternative or "addendum" to more traditional psychoanalytic theory. RET was developed in clinical work with adult patients. However, in recent years there has been an interest in RET principles for children culminating in Rational Education —an intriguing concept that merited attention in this volume.

Transactional Analysis (TA) was chosen in part because it is apparently easily understood by most individuals, thus making the approach significant in terms of social effectiveness. As will be discussed below, a large number of catastrophes in the disciplinary dyad result from crossed transactions and/or negotiations from the wrong ego states. TA offers a rapid way of identifying destructive disciplinary transactions and suggests ways to avoid them.

The views of Haim Ginott do not constitute a theory. However, Ginott, the practical clinician, made major contributions to our understanding of ways to deal with the disciplinary interaction in a constructive manner. His works are remarkably practical and deserved a place in this format.

Perhaps more than any other group, the behaviorists have addressed problems that are typically "disciplinary" — for example, toothbrushing, homework, arguing, fighting. Though often criticized, the work of the behaviorists is precise, methodical, and practical. Further, the vigorous debates that have raged between psychoanalysts and cognitive theorists on the one hand and behaviorists on the other made it imperative that the behavioral approach be included in a book on discipline.

In our attempts to accede to pragmatism, we were forced to omit several points of view that potentially have much to say about the subject of discipline. The most obvious are the works of the Adlerians, such as Dreikurs (1950), and Gordon's (1970) Parent Effectiveness Training. Erikson's (1950) and Sullivan's (1953) theories regarding psychosocial development are also relevant.

To ensure proper representation, each point of view is presented by recognized authorities. While a specialist, each participant is dedicated to the principle that dialogue facilitates the attainment of knowledge. The volume is intended for a wide array of mental health and educational professionals. Since it is expected that many readers will not have an extensive background in psychology, each chapter provides a review of fundamental principles of the theory in question that are relevant to issues of child management and discipline. Following this review of basics, specific applications of the theory to the problem of discipline are discussed together with practical suggestions.

We hope that the reader, thus provided with a spectrum of views regarding child management and discipline, can make a fair analysis of and comparison among these views as they relate to his or her particular social context. The way in which one goes about choosing a point of view is something of a mystery. Probably the biases that pervade one's training and one's philosophical world view (Messer and Winokur, 1980) are as significant in making this choice as are the preferred theory's data base and logical structure. Yet it would seem wisest to make a choice on the basis of the theory or theory's utility to the individual.

Relevant factors would include the demands of the setting, the characteristics of the youngsters being worked with, the amount of time available, the role and goals of the worker, and the personal ease with which the worker can adopt and use the point of view.

Our approach to these issues obviously promotes the spirit of eclecticism. Because the exigencies of service usually demand pragmatism, eclecticism is generally tolerated in applied settings yet must be often defended in academic circles. For example, Henle (1957) charged that in accepting the good features of various theories, the eclectic is likely to blur the contradictory differences among them. Marx and Hillix (1963) argued that since theories are intended in part to provide us with systems for deducing statements from empirical data, eclecticism may lead us between the deductive strengths of respective theories, thus weakening our conceptual-predictive potency. While Marx and Hillix admitted that some forms of eclecticism may be acceptable, they warned that "the eclectic misses some of the stimulation, as well as the acrimony, of controversy; his temperament will determine whether or not this is good" (p. 103).

Marx and Hillix's conclusion highlights a central difficulty with "antieclecticism." A major purpose of a psychological conceptual system is to guide us in our efforts to understand and assist people, not to provide us with a foolproof system for debate. While a particular theory may have merit, in most cases an integration of the helpful aspects of each point of view may provide a richer source of guidance for the applied worker. Indeed, Bandura's (1978) work on reciprocal determinism suggests that a broader, more integrative point of view may be coming into favor among researchers as well.

No attempt has been made to influence how the reader integrates the material contained in this work. However, to facilitate comparison, contrast, and integration, a final chapter has been prepared in which the contributions of each of the points of view are discussed in the context of clinical cases. To ensure accuracy, each author reviewed the case materials. No final metatheory is presented, although an attempt has been made to highlight the ways in which each approach may be helpful. This work is not seen as the alpha and omega of the study of discipline. Rather, it is our purpose to legitimize attention to the subject of discipline and to stimulate further dialogue among proponents of various points of view regarding discipline as well as other socially meaningful problems.

REFERENCES

Bakan, D. (1971), *Slaughter of the Innocents.* San Francisco: Jossey-Bass.

Bandura, A. (1978), The self system in reciprocal determinism. *American Psychologist*, 33:344–358.

Baumrind, D. (1966), Effects of authoritative parental control on child behavior. *Child Development*, 37:887–907.

_____ (1967), Child care practices anteceding three patterns of preschool behavior. *Genetic Psychol.*, 75:43–88.

_____ (1968), Authoritarian vs. authoritative parental control. *Adolescence*, 3:255–272.

_____ (1971a), Harmonious parents and their preschool children. *Dev. Psychol.*, 4:99–102.

_____ (1971b), Current patterns of parental authority. *Dev. Psychol.*, 4(1, part 2):1–103.

_____ (1975), The contributions of the family to the development of competence in children. *Schizophrenia Bull.*, 1: 12–37.

Becker, W. C. (1964), Consequences of different kinds of parental discipline. In: *Review of Child Development Research*, Vol. 1, ed. M. L. Hoffman and L. W. Hoffman. New York: Russell Sage, pp. 169–208.

Child Abuse Prevention Act (1973), S. 1911 (93rd Congress, 1st Session, March 26).

Comenius, J. A. (1653), *The School of Infancy*. Edited and translated by E. M. Eller. Chapel Hill: The University of North Carolina Press, 1956.

Coopersmith, S. (1968), Studies in self-esteem. *Scientific American*, 218:96–102.

Deur, J. I., and Parke, R. D. (1970), Effects of inconsistent punishment on aggression in children. *Dev. Psychol.*, 2: 403–411.

Dobson, J. (1970), *Dare to Discipline*. Wheaton, Ill.: Tyndale House.

Dreikurs, R. (1950), *Fundamentals of Adlerian Psychology*. New York: Greenberg.

Erikson, E. H. (1950), *Childhood and Society*. New York: Norton.

Gil, D. G. (1970), *Violence Against Children: Physical Child Abuse in the United States*. Cambridge, Mass.: Harvard University Press.

Gordon, T. (1970), *Parent Effectiveness Training: The Tested New Way to Raise Responsible Children*. New York: McKay.

Henle, M. (1957), Some problems of eclecticism. *Psychological Rev.*, 64:296–305.

Kempe, C. H., and Helfer, R. E., Eds. (1972), *Helping the Battered Child and His Family*. New York: Lippincott.

Lasch, C. (1979), *The Culture of Narcissism: American Life in an Age of Diminishing Expectations*. New York: Norton.

Levine, M., and Levine, A. (1970), *A Social History of the Helping Services*. New York: Appleton-Century-Crofts.

Marx, M. H., and Hillix, W. A. (1963), *Systems and Theories of Psychology*. New York: McGraw-Hill.

McCord, W., McCord, J., and Zola, I. K. (1959), *Origins of Crime*. New York: Columbia University Press.

Messer, S. B., and Winokur, M. (1980), Some limits to the integration of psychoanalytic and behavior therapy. *Amer. Psychologist*, 35:818–827.

Neill, A. S. (1960), *Summerhill: A Radical Approach to Child Rearing*. New York: Hart.

Pollack, J. H. (1968), Five frequent mistakes of parents. *Today's Health*, 46:14–29.

Rosenthal, M. J. (1962), The syndrome of the inconsistent mother. *Amer. J. of Ortho.*, 32:637–644.

Schvaneveldt, J. D., Freyer, M., and Ostler, R. (1970), Concept of "badness" and "goodness" of parents as perceived by nursery school children. *Family Coordinator*, 19:98–103.

Sears, R. R. (1961), Relation of early socialization experiences to aggression in middle childhood. *J. of Abnor. and Soc. Psychol.*, 63:466–492.

———, Maccoby, E. E., and Levin, H. (1957), *Patterns of Child Rearing*. Evanston, Ill.: Row, Peterson.

Spinetta, J. J., and Rigler, D. (1972), The child abusing parent: Psychological review. *Psychological Bull.*, 77:296–304.

Spock, B. (1974), *Raising Children in a Difficult Time*. New York: Norton.

Sullivan, H. S. (1953), *The Interpersonal Theory of Psychiatry*, New York: Norton.

Winder, C. L., and Rau, L. (1962), Parental attitudes associated with social deviance in preadolescent boys. *J. of Abnor. and Soc. Psychol.*, 64:418–424.

World Health Organization (1962), *Deprivation of maternal care: A reassessment of its effects*. Geneva.

2

Discipline from the Psychoanalytic Viewpoint

Loretta K. Cass, Ph.D.

Early in its history, psychoanalysis addressed itself to discipline only indirectly, as part of its developmental approach to personality, specifically to the effects of parent-child relationships early in the life of the child. Freud spoke of discipline in relation to the development of "conscience," a gradual process of internalization of parental rules and prohibitions during the preschool years, but he attributed this process only in part to the child's *real* experience of his parents' behavior and attitudes toward him. The child's conscience represented, as well, his fantasies about the powerful parent, fantasies based on the "collective unconscious" of generations past. It is this latter belief of psychoanalytic theory which has attracted the strongest criticism. Critics have equated Freud's position on morality with the religious concept "original sin" and have tried to relegate the whole theory to the limbo of untestable hypotheses.

Although the idea of conscience as a *structure* may be untestable, the *process* to which Freud attributed the formation of conscience, that is, internalization, has been the subject of much modern-day research and is generally acknowledged to be the ultimate goal in socialization. Thus Selma Fraiberg, in her very practical work on the problems of early childhood, *The Magic Years*, holds that socialization depends upon the success of internalization: "The acquisition of standards of behavior, the restriction of impulses and urges, will not develop without teaching. . . . [The child] has no incentives of his own, no inherited tendencies 'to be good,' to be unselfish, to control his appetites and his temper. His parents provide the incentives and much later in his development the child will call these incentives his own" (1959, p. 146). A "good conscience" in these modern neoanalytic terms is taken out of the realm of mysticism and becomes simply a descriptive term for an internal system "that can regulate and control the primary human drives according to the requirements of society" (Fraiberg, 1959, p. 243). It is built, not inherited; learned, not given; and it depends upon the actual or imagined relationships between the child and those closest to him. How well and how quickly conscience develops is dependent upon the progress of other acquisitions, such as cognition, affect, and object relationships.

    The way in which human beings learn or fail to learn "to control the primary human drives according to the requirements of society" is embedded in psychoanalysis's theory of personality development (S. Freud, 1933; Hartmann, 1960). The theory is essentially a dynamic one, the main assumption of which is that the *process* of personality construction in an individual is the history of the fate of need gratification. The story of a personality can be traced in the way that needs are expressed or inhibited, in reactions to their deprivation and frustration, and in the success or failure in accommodating to the demands of reality in need expression. Freud talked of need gratification as the "purpose and intention of life as shown in man's behavior." His definition of happiness was simply "an absence of pain and unpleasure and. . . the experiencing of strong feelings of pleasure" (1930, p. 76). He called this most basic assumption "the pleasure principle" and held that "this principle dominates the operation of the mental apparatus from the start." Freud's pessimism arose out of his conviction that this goal of happiness has "no possibility" of realization; "all the regulations of the universe run counter to it." For while the very nature of need gratification and protection from outside dangers requires the presence and cooperation of other people, living with them sets up the requirement to regulate the relationships among people. "If the attempt were not made, the relationships would be subject to the arbitrary will of the individual: that is to say, the physically stronger man would decide them in the sense of his own interests and instinctual impulses. . . . Human life in common is only made possible when a majority comes together which is stronger than any separate individual and which remains united against all separate individuals. . . . This replacement of the power of the individual by the power of a community constitutes the decisive step of civilization" (Freud, 1930, p. 95). Freud saw the family as the operational unit of civilization and he drew an analogy between the development of an individual within a family and the development of civilization. Most children's first need gratifications, as well as their first frustrations, are provided by their families; later, "society" plays its part in providing a long succession of gratifications, regulations, and deprivations.

While most recent theorists agree with Freud on the preeminence of need gratification in the dynamics of personality and on the inevitability of frustration, they do not always agree with him on personal happiness as the criterion for mental health. Thus, Fraiberg holds that "mental health must be judged not only by the relative harmony that prevails within the human ego, but by the requirements of a civilized people for the attainment of the highest social values" (1959, p. 7). Most analysts accept frustration and anxiety as expected consequences of the limitations of the human condition (especially in childhood) and of the restrictions inherent in socialization. But instead of bewailing the lost paradise of instinctual freedom, many now stress the survival and social values of anxiety and the motivational role of frustration in the process of learning (e.g., Hartmann and Lowenstein, 1962).

Within this complex, gradual evolution from a helpless, impulse-determined infant to a socialized, ego-directed adult, the importance of the individual with his inherited and acquired assets and liabilities cannot be separated from that of the forces around him which participate, for better or worse, in his socialization. Psychoanalysis holds that there is an inherent and fairly consistent sequence of psychosexual stages with one form of sexuality (drive) ascendant at each stage, but with wide individual differences in the intensity and mode of expression of these drives. The stages reflect the body zones — that is, the oral, anal, and phallic zones. For the human, interpersonal relationships seem to be the greatest external influence on the expression of drives. As a child advances through the psychosexual stage, parents and immediate family are his first and closest socializers and thus, according to analytic theory, influence the process most. But as maturity increases, other agents become increasingly influential (A. Freud, 1974).

In one sense, psychoanalysis summarizes its personality theory within its views on the fate of impulse and need expression in the life of an individual; thus, the subject of impulse control and, consequently, of discipline, permeates the theory. There are specific principles of analytic theory, however, which have direct application to discipline.

PSYCHOANALYTIC POSTULATES BASIC TO ITS VIEW OF DISCIPLINE

1. Psychoanalysis is a developmental theory; any one area of development, such as moral or social development, occurs in sequential stages, each dependent on progress through the stage preceding. Moreover, development within one area is greatly affected by that in other areas, so that, for example, the development of "conscience" is dependent on an increase in cognitive skills, such as forethought and the capacity for empathy, on the learning of impulse control, on psychosexual advancement, and on changes in object relationships.

2. Experiences early in life have a primary advantage in influencing character development. This effect derives from the helplessness of the human infant, which makes him highly susceptible to the influence of the agents of his need gratification, especially where nurturance and the relief of tension and discomfort are concerned. The importance of these early experiences leads directly to a third assumption.

3. Parental influence usually outweighs that of other agencies in the child's life. Because of both the primacy in time of their interactions with the child and the affect involved, parents play a prominent role in the internalization of rules and inhibitions, whether these are of a socially constructive or destructive nature. (The internalization of socially destructive attitudes is too often neglected in research on internalization.)

4. Much of early character development occurs un-

consciously, often before cognition is sufficiently developed to be used—in fact, to be *useable*—by those who would discipline the child. Early reactions of anxiety, such as that associated with separation from the mother or that with punishment, may not be consciously integrated by the child or subjected to cause-and-effect logic, but are, nevertheless, extremely important in terms of conditioning so that later experiences may be responded to on the basis of this early consequence rather than on current expectations.

5. Psychoanalytic theory stresses the importance of guilt in the process of internalization. Freud described the creation of conscience as a gradual and painful one. The child gives up his wishes to do what he pleases, when he pleases, because of external forces. "First comes renunciation of instinct owing to fear of aggression by the *external* authority. . . . After that comes the erection of an *internal* authority, and renunciation of instinct owing to fear of it—owing to fear of conscience. In this second situation, bad intentions are equated with bad actions, and hence come a sense of guilt and a need for punishment. The aggressiveness of the conscience keeps up the aggressiveness of authority" (1930, p. 128). In discussing this second process, Freud describes what is so apparent in many conforming, but still guilty, children: that the severity of their conscience may not correspond at all to the severity of the parental treatment they have received. Their anxiety is based on a conscience more punitive than any external authority.

6. Identification is the vehicle for the internalization of external authority, and it is this process through which rules and prohibitions get from outside to inside the child, that is, are internalized (Malmquist, 1968, pp. 304 ff.). Angered and frustrated by restrictions and deprivations, but unable to overcome the more powerful parent, the

child takes on his characteristics, becomes *like* the parent and, in the process, takes on the authority role toward his own behavior. Freud thought of this as a unitary and comprehensive takeover and stressed the negative (aggressive) aspects of identification. "By means of identification he takes the unattackable authority into himself. The authority now turns into his superego and enters into possession of all the aggressiveness which a child would have liked to exercise against it" (1930, p. 129). But Freud also included love in the process of identification: "His sons hated him (the father) but they loved him, too" (1930, p. 132). Anaclitic identification, which is based on the child's *love* of his parents and his anxiety when he loses it or fears its loss, results in the child's becoming like the parent in ways other than that of authority alone. Neoanalytic theorists have stressed the young child's replacing early fantasies of his own omnipotence with the idealization of his parents and then sharing, through identification, in their ideals. These ideals also become part of the self, that is, form the ego-ideal (Lampl-de Groot, 1962).

7. Analytic theory stresses the importance of *transference* in the child's reactions to extrafamilial authority figures. In its stress on the primacy effect of early (parent-child) interactions, psychoanalysis initially offered a rather pessimistic outlook for later changes in character structure through outside agents. Indeed, Freud spoke of the inevitable conflict that "is set going as soon as men are faced with the task of living together. . . . What began in relation to the father is completed in relation to the group. If civilization is a necessary course of development from the family to humanity as a whole then . . . there is inextricably bound up with it an increase in the sense of guilt" (1930, pp. 132–133). Certainly, the power of parental influence has been confirmed in research and is well known

to every school teacher. The child comes to school with learned reactions to authority and transfers these and his expectation onto the teacher. Often the teacher is faced with transference of negative attitudes which she had no part in creating.

Newer psychoanalytic theory does not subscribe so generally to Freud's fatalism. Selma Fraiberg, for example, while agreeing to the unmistakable importance of the early years, cites as a fallacy the concept of "Childhood as Destiny," that is, "the belief that the experiences of early childhood determine one's fate. . . . For while the experiences of early childhood provide the *foundations* for personality development, there is no way of predicting in early childhood how these experiences will influence personality development" (1959, p. 286). Follow-up of children into adulthood points up the complexity of personality determinants.

8. Finally, psychoanalytic theory emphasizes the importance of a child's fantasy and how it leads to distortion of real situations. Perhaps this is the significant difference between psychoanalytic and behavioristic theories of personality when it comes to practical application. For if psychoanalytic theory is correct, it suggests that *understanding* what is going on in the child's mind may be crucial in deciding what sort of discipline is appropriate. This is the thrust of the currently popular encouragement of better communication between adults and children; if the child lives by his fantasy, the adult may often operate upon wholly incorrect premises about the bases of the child's overt behavior.

IMPLICATIONS FOR
THE APPLICATION OF DISCIPLINE

Freud had very little to say about any specific techniques through which internalization might be promoted.

The child, by nature of his status in the family, runs up against the rules and restrictions of the parents, real or imagined; out of anger, fear, or love he learns to respond to the powerful parents' demands and, finally, to take these on as his own internal controls. Freud saw this process as beginning in infancy and normally reaching actual internalization with the resolution of the oedipal conflict.

Several later analytic writers, such as Anna Freud (1974) and Selma Fraiberg (1959), have taken Freud's theory, modified it, and applied it to discipline which, to Fraiberg, is simply "education of the child for self-control" (p. 244). As an application of psychoanalytic theory, discipline should be suited differentially to developmental stages; it should not become a blind reaction to immature attitudes or expectations that a child has transferred from parents onto other authority figures; it should not represent the disciplinarian's hostilities and conflicts from his own past; it should assess and take into account the *real* basis for the child's behavior, a basis which may relate more to his fantasies than to the actualities of the situation.

The Importance of Understanding

The focus in most of the recent analytic literature on the upbringing of children is on the need for understanding the child through his behavior. Discipline which does not take understanding into account can be, at the least, ineffectual, and, at the worst, destructive. Too often, the adult simply reacts to a particular behavior according to what he sees or hears, or according to what it awakens in him, without making the effort to know what might be occurring within the child. In our hurried and event-crowded daily life, the quickest and easiest response to misbehavior is to yell or punish and think about it later, if at all. To respond instead with understanding would require: (1) some knowledge of where this particular child is in his development — that is, what level he has reached in the capacity for impulse control, the meaning of specific relationships, etc.; (2) what kinds of intervention are effective for this particular child; and (3) what may be going on just now that has brought on the behavior so that the response can be addressed to the cause of the behavior. Understanding requires learning to listen and to hear the *message* in behavior, a message which may be directly opposite or only distantly related to what the child is doing. Take, for example, the child whose outward aggression toward other children is his means of counteracting a deathly fear of being injured. The adult must prohibit the acting out of his aggression, but must also recognize and help alleviate the fear for which the child's aggression is a defense. Telling the child that we understand how he feels and that people often strike out in anger when they are upset will often do wonders to foster a relationship in which the child can begin to bring out his feelings and work on them instead of on the people around him.

> Three-year-old David was extremely upset because his parents were leaving him with a baby-sitter one evening. He was screaming at the top of his lungs and calling his parents every bad name he could think of. Dad reacted with anger, came back and began to spank David. The baby-sitter was a mature woman who understood what David, at three, was going through in relation to his feelings of jealousy toward his father and grief over his mother's leaving him and who knew that Dad's spanking could only add to David's hostility toward the more powerful father. She asked the father not to spank him. After the parents had gone she held David close and talked

to him about how he might be feeling, and also reassured him that he would be all right with her and that his parents would come back soon. David calmed down. He had found that somebody understood how awful he felt, and that in itself made the feeling tolerable.

The challenge of discipline based on understanding may, at first, seem wholly impossible to meet, especially in a classroom of twenty to forty children or in a daycare or residential center. It is an ideal which seems to require attention to and interaction with one child at a time. Even the teacher who is knowledgeable about child development and the dynamics underlying behavior may despair of applying her knowledge when she has to deal with a group.

And yet the picture in the schoolroom or in other group settings is not as hopeless as it would seem. There *are* certain principles arising out of psychoanalytic theory that can be applied constructively to most children in the socialization process and that are not likely to be destructive to the few unusual children in the group. For example, children need, and will come to welcome, structure, especially where their young age or inherent inadequacies render them vulnerable to the loss of control. When discipline is a kindly imposition of structure through rules and positive reinforcement, nearly *all* children can respond to and benefit from it. A summary of the results of parent-children research on power-assertive discipline (physical punishment, deprivation of privileges, or the application or threat of force) as compared with love-oriented techniques and with induction (giving the child reasons for changing his behavior) indicates that power-assertive discipline is associated with weak moral development (Hoffman, 1970, p. 292). When a teacher has applied positive approaches to a group, she needs still to be alert to those few children who do not respond to the expectable, to consider the reasons why, and to adapt to these children's singular needs. Over the period of a school year, there is ample occasion to observe and to try to understand the unusual child. He will repeat in many different contexts the same message and the adult who listens can usually hear what it is.

Discipline Consistent with Developmental Theory

Practically all approaches to discipline recognize the importance of age difference in the techniques to be employed. Disciplining a two-year-old must be in terms of concrete, structured, immediate interventions, and rules must be simple and definite (e.g., Kohlberg, 1964; Stone and Church, 1968). Although discipline for this age level has many of the characteristics of simple conditioning and there is little chance for supplying verbal cause-and-effect information, the importance of the parents' *affect* in these early interactions is greater than at any time thereafter. Not as yet able to understand an angry parental outburst and having developed very little defense against anxiety, the child is likely to feel overwhelmed and helpless and this experience may well condition his reactions to subsequent adult interventions. The question of spanking at young ages is pertinent here. Inflicting physical pain may be effective in terms of stopping undesirable behavior, and equally effective in destroying a positive relationship to the adult (Whiting and Child, 1953).

The two-year-old often gets into trouble because of his need to explore and handle everything he can reach and because of his resistance to being controlled. Both of these characteristics are "natural" steps in his growth toward autonomy, but when they are acted out day in and day out, they try the patience of even the most understanding parent. Some parents find themselves in a constant struggle to protect their valuables from being broken. Others have put everything that is at once valuable and movable away in order to avoid the struggle. Taking into account the developmental stage at two (that control is still largely on an external basis and that the two-year-old may not be able to understand explanations as to why he can't have those things he wants so much), the best course of discipline is usually one that minimizes the necessity for restrictions and plays them in a low key when they become necessary. Specifically, this means arranging the environment with as few temptations as possible for the toddler, but creating one place where he can handle and bang things to his heart's content; it also means saying "no" firmly but quietly and removing him from those things that can't be his. Within a few years, he will be more willing to listen and more able to understand cause-and-effect explanations if he hasn't previously been subjected to whipping that could only seem, at age two, to be an attack by a fearsome giant.

The five- or six-year-old has more capacity for control and the inestimable advantage of language. Discipline may now include talking about the situation and encouraging forethought. If things have gone reasonably well in the oedipal period just past, a boy will have given up the fantasy, at least for a while, that he can replace his father, and his sister will have learned that mother is here to stay.

Other reality is here to stay, too, and it gradually takes on a fascination that will keep most children busy for many years to come. Now they want to know the *reason* for everything. Even school is fun if it is arranged to correspond to their capacities and to encourage rather than to stifle their curiosity. Now the task of socialization is to capitalize on the reality-orientation of the stage. The six-year-old can be told the reasons for rules and understand the logic of cause and effect, even when the effect may be simply that the behavior is disturbing to others and they have a right not to be disturbed. Moreover, the six-year-old can *talk* more freely about the things inside himself. He can learn to talk about his problems and about alternate ways to cope with them.

Margie had been causing trouble at school all week. She came in each morning ready to pick a fight with any child in her class who happened to be in her way. She wouldn't pay attention to the teacher but kept demanding attention for herself until finally the whole class was in an uproar. One day toward the end of the week, the teacher, in desperation, was just about to send Margie out of the room but then stopped to consider how she might handle the situation in a way that could help Margie and the other children to learn from it. She told the children that she thought they all needed to talk about what had been going on all week in the room. Maybe they could figure out together how to make things better. The children were reticent at first, but with encouragement they said what they thought was wrong and how they felt about it. The teacher made sure that Margie was not made the scapegoat by encouraging her to talk, too, and by having them all face their individual responsibility for what had happened. After that, the teacher asked for suggestions as to what could be done so the class could go on and do its work. She was surprised at the realistic solutions the children came up with: Have Margie sit near to the teacher until she feels better; let Mary (who was way ahead in her work) sit at a separate table with Margie and help her catch up with her work; help Margie to see that she would have to stop picking on other kids if she wanted them to like her, etc. Instead of leaving the room to spend her time sitting in the principal's office and brooding, Margie had been given the opportunity to face the reality of how she affected other people and, more importantly, to feel their concern for her.

The early school years, called the "latency years" by Freud because of the relative submergence of the sexual drives of the oedipal period, present the optimal conditions for socialization. Ideally, having dealt with his oedipal fantasy and been forced to accept the reality of his position in the family, the child learns that by modeling after the parent of the same sex, he can gain both parents' approval. He turns from the anxiety of family closeness to the safety of formal learning, and, for most children, learning soon becomes rewarding in its own right. Since this is the golden age for reality testing and the development of reason and logic, the latency stage, more than all others, sets the tone and limits for conformity. By the same token, the child who will not give in to regulations, especially at school, is now singled out. More children are referred to child guidance clinics during the early grades than at other ages and the reason for referral is predominantly school "misbehavior." But for the vast majority of children, it is the time for internalization, for solidifying the superego. Freud relates the establishment of true superego to the resolution of the oedipal conflict and to identification with the parents of the same sex. Now the child seeks this parent's approval of his behavior and gradually turns to those outside the home, to teachers and peers, for their approval too.

The problem of control surges again in adolescence when the equilibrium between ego and id attained during latency is upset through the stress of insistent sexual and aggressive drives. Even conforming children may become

punitive way, anxiety disappears, and its potential for internalization has been wasted. If instead, discipline is applied through induction (the use of reasons for a change in behavior), both the effects of guilt and the conceptualization of cause-and-effect relationships operate in favor of internalization. With a stage-appropriate increase in the capacity for empathy, the adolescent can be led to think about the effect of his actions on others, and the scales may be tipped in favor of giving up behavior based on gratification of egocentric drives.

Sometimes the need to punish the self is so great that no ordinary means are sufficient to block its expression. Adolescents in therapy sometimes can talk about this tremendous force, but often it is only after they have engaged in self-destructive behavior of some kind. Here the process of internalization has been a negative one, that is, the external punishing force has become part of the self but operates to destroy rather than to enhance its growth.

Debbie was in a weekly therapy group with four other adolescent girls for over a year. She had been brought to the clinic by her step-father who openly stated that he was afraid he would "beat her to death" if she kept on with her defiance and sexual acting out. She had entertained, and often shocked, the other girls with accounts of her sexual escapades, which she seemed to treat lightly and as proof of her sophistication and freedom. The other girls, as "socializers" are apt to do, tried to warn Debbie of the consequences of her actions: She might become pregnant; she was losing her friends; her parents were threatening to kick her out of the house; she wouldn't be wanted by "decent" fellows, etc. Debbie countered their reasoning: she knew how to take care of herself; she had nothing to lose at home where her step-father had mistreated her sexually several times until she got "wise" to him; she had made new friends that she liked better than the "squares" she used to go around with. Debbie obviously liked the therapist but her interpretations of what Debbie was acting out were as ineffective as those of the adolescents in the group. Debbie stayed another year in therapy, then disappeared, leaving the group and her home suddenly.

Ten years later Debbie came back to see the therapist. She was now happily married and had two children, one from a present marriage and another from her first marriage. Debbie wanted to tell the therapist that she had known what the therapist was saying to her in the group sessions. She had recognized the truth of the therapist's interpretations — that she seemed to be very guilty and was punishing herself through her behavior. She recalled, too, how much she had needed and wanted the therapist's help but how she felt she could never leave herself vulnerable to another adult, who, like her father and step-father, might betray her trust. Even though she had come to understand something about herself, she was driven for several years to get herself into trouble. She had run off with a soldier who was AWOL, had worked to support the two of them, and had stayed with him even though he abused her physically. They had one child, but it was when her husband's physical abuse caused her to lose a baby in her second pregnancy that Debbie decided she had had enough. She could finally call a halt to the punishment and move out and up from her degradation. After she divorced her husband, Debbie spent the next few years working, taking good care of her little boy, and gaining, in the process, a belated sense of self-worth and identity. Later she could enter into a marriage based on mutual respect.

With the development of the cognitive ability to abstract and conceptualize, children learn to imagine themselves "in the other person's shoes" and, thus, to empathize with the other's feelings and problems. The capacity for empathy is especially notable in adolescence and occurs right alongside the egocentrism that accompanies a sense of personal identity and individuality. Adolescents are highly susceptible to "causes" and will work hard for them, often to the detriment of working toward their own careers. Recently, the cause of the rights of others, especially of the disadvantaged, has won the support of adolescent groups. Adults, especially of the older generation, have complained that adolescents' fervor to protect others' rights hasn't included the rights of the parents who pay the bills, the teachers who are trying to educate them, or the police who may have to interfere with their activities. Often this conflict pits adolescents against "authority" in open warfare and disciplinary measures are instituted. As recent history has demonstrated, tragedy may then ensue, either in the form of destructive confrontation or, unfortunately, the extinction of the adolescents' noble efforts to change society's treatment of its oppressed peoples. Adults must understand that adolescents in their ambivalent need to assert their independence from those *closest* in their daily lives must rebel against *them* and substitute more distant people to love. Their choice to espouse underprivileged groups may be their way of vicariously overcoming the inferior status they feel in relation to their privileged parents. The importance of what one feels or imagines to be, rather than what may actually be the case, is clearly illustrated in this perennial conflict between generations. The parent may feel or even may actually be physically or educationally inferior to his adolescent offspring all the while the adolescent is feeling extremely jealous of his "superior" parent. Once understood, such feelings and thoughts can be communicated from one generation to the other, although the communication is very difficult while passions are at their height.

It is significant that as the adolescent moves beyond his involvement with his family to find his mate and establish his own home, he can usually look back on this conflict and wonder at the intensity of his past feelings. Again, he learns through experience, often dearly bought, to internalize a set of values that, while bearing some similarity to those of his parents, are more truly now his own. When internalization has been successful, sublimation of instinctual drives into vocational, artistic, and intellectual achievement results. Civilization rests upon the relative success of sublimation in its individual members.

Parental Influence Including Transference

The hope for success in discipline during school years is inextricably bound up with progress in the building of conscience before that time. Conscience doesn't just "happen" at six or seven years of age (Malmquist, 1968). The five-year-old is just beginning to be his own disciplinarian, and with the best of parenting, the changeover from external control of behavior to internalized ideals and standards is a slow and tedious one. If through their love, they have been successful in making their approval important to the child, parents are likely to watch a gradual identification with themselves, usually on a like-sex basis, and a corresponding imitation of their rules and prohibitions, with less latitude than they would allow. At first, the conformity still requires the presence of, or at least the *thought* of the presence of, the parents. It is usually not until the late stages of adolescence or early

adulthood that the standards are truly part of the self and
no longer require the presence or thought of the parent.
Research by Loevinger and Wessler (1970) indicates that
a large portion of our society never reach this final goal.

Educators are faced with the question of their responsibility in the continuing process of building conscience in other people's children. Children come to them
in various stages of the process. At worst they may be far
behind the norm for their age level, and the teacher is
likely to be pressed into the role of external force.

An experience while I was consulting with a group
of teachers in a city grade school illustrates this
point. I had been meeting weekly with eight teachers
over a period of a few months, when one Monday
morning I had an urgent telephone call from the
principal asking if I could come to the school within
the hour since he had called an emergency meeting of
all the parents of children in a "special" class for the
mildly retarded. I arrived at the school to find some
twenty-five parents assembled on one side of the
classroom and some thirty children, all boys, on the
other, with the principal and a teacher in between.
That in itself was a sight to behold, but what was
really a shock was the condition of the room. It was
in utter chaos. All the books had been torn up and
thrown about the room, the shades were in shreds,
the doors of the cabinets were torn from their hinges,
and all the furniture that could be moved had been
overturned. Naturally my first thought was what
could have brought on such chaos. The parents had
been called from their jobs and, except for a few vo-
ciferous and hostile ones, looked bewildered and
frightened. The children were mainly quiet except for
some snickering and whispering to one another.

I listened as one irate father attacked the teacher

for not being able to "control these kids—all you have to do is let them know that you're the boss. I'd get a strap and use it every day if I had to—that's what Larry gets at home." (It turned out that Larry had been one of the ringleaders in tearing up the room.) After a while I edged myself into the verbal interchange and suggested that we might ask the children what had happened. With much encouragement, they told us how angry they were because they had lost their shop teacher and their "shop" along with him. Their shop tools were all locked in cabinets, and the children were supposed to sit and learn from the books that only a few of them could read. When, on that Monday morning, Larry had shouted out, "Let's get those saws and hammers," the teacher was powerless to stop the destruction.

For those children who are working on internalization, the teacher becomes an important parental substitute and can facilitate or retard the process. Imposing external force, whether in terms of material reinforcement or of punishment, may get quick results. The "traditional" schoolroom with its fear of the teacher has been held up even by parents as a model to which educators should return. Society has bestowed upon parents "dominant status" rights over their children, and this power is passed on through each new generation. Most parents argue that they have the right to use corporal punishment because their children "belong" to them and many parents are only too willing to grant this "right," in turn, to the schools. Yet the weight of research evidence is that aggression by adults toward children begets aggression in children. They model after parents and teachers, and so it is, in our culture, that the vicious cycle of aggression is perpetuated (Bandura and Walters, 1963). But, if the goal of society is to develop trusting and self-regulating individuals who care about the welfare of others as well as their own, the responsibility of educators must not simply be to have order in the classroom, but to use those methods of discipline which promote the development of self-control and social conscience. Techniques other than force have been shown to be effective. Especially encouraging have been the findings on "other-oriented induction" — the technique of pointing out to the child the implications of his behavior for another person (Hoffman, 1970, pp. 282–327).

One difficulty in this task is that every child, especially a young one, will generalize (transfer) from his parent to his teacher or other caretaker. Expecting punishment, for example, he will try to get it. Expecting overindulgence, he will be devastated if he meets firmness instead. The teacher doesn't need to act out these expectations, however, and it is exactly in not carrying out immature parental behavior that she helps the child to seek new ways of coping — new and better ways to gain approval, this time from teacher to student. When the standards are accompanied by discussion of *why* they are necessary, the stage is set for incorporation of the new authority inside the child.

Children of school age are capable of discussing things that happen in the classroom, looking at reasons for behavior, and offering better ways to behave. This discussion technique is little used even though it has a dual advantage of getting children involved in a *cognitive* way in their own immediate interacting and, through this *internal* thought process, of promoting useable concepts and principles for the future. *Thinking* and *talking* about feelings and relationships are too infrequently used as a substitute for action.

One sixth grade class was put into turmoil every few weeks when Randy, after one of his regular absences, would return to class and begin to demand special attention. He was new in the room that year and his unkempt appearance and poor use of language set him apart from his classmates. He had become the scapegoat of the class. The teacher found it increasingly difficult to maintain discipline on these occasions and decided to bring the matter to the class while Randy was absent. She began by asking what the children thought might be possible reasons for Randy's absences. After various guesses, one child came up with a reason very near the real one — that his parents traveled and took him along. Actually, they were entertainers who went on out-of-town engagements. Then the class discussed why he might be so far behind in class and how this might make him feel. Once they began to realize what a difficult time Randy was having, the children were asking how they could *help* him when he returned. They learned a valuable lesson in caring for another human being and the teacher's discipline problem was alleviated.

THE NEED FOR SELF-UNDERSTANDING

"Discipline" is usually thought of as a one-way street: what a person in authority does to another person to teach conformity or develop self-control. Little attention is paid to the characteristics and feelings of the disciplinarians as they relate to the process. Just as children are the products of their endowment and their life experience, so also the adults who would discipline them carry over feelings and distortions from their past. Often these hang-ups set the tone for discipline in general and for the kind of relationship to certain behaviors or particular "kinds" of children. No one is free of such subjective influences. The best that can be hoped for is some understanding of one's own tendencies to overreact to certain misbehaviors, as when, for example, the disciplinarian sees in a particular child some hated rival from the past and treats the child accordingly.

After some five months of weekly meetings for a group of grade-school teachers, it became apparent to all of us but the teacher concerned that her dislike for one aggressive boy was more than his behavior warranted and, more importantly, that her handling of the situation had involved the two of them in a pitched battle with no truce in sight. Fortunately, her unconscious took over as we discussed the problem and she suddenly blurted out that the boy looked just like her younger brother! She stopped and blushed, and, for an uneasy minute, dead silence prevailed. Suddenly we all laughed and we all knew that she had just free-associated into a valuable bit of insight, which, in the weeks to come, wholly revamped her handling of the problem.

Such insights are usually not easy to come by. Rare is the person who, outside of the therapeutic relationship, can face his own unresolved conflicts and see how they operate to distort his current perceptions and reactions. The extremes of these distortions are represented in the horrors of child abuse. While there are, as yet, no firm conclusions as to which causal variables predominate among the many that have been presented to account for the high rate of child abuse in the United States, there is good data to support the view that parents, teachers, and other caretakers often mistreat children as an outgrowth of their own dynamics (Gil, 1970). Such abuse, often righteously administered under the name of "discipline," may simply serve to relieve the adult's uncontrollable anger or tension and have little to do with the "offense" alleged. In other instances, it is an unmistakable projection of some specific conflict that the child abuser has never resolved. For example, a woman may project hatred for her late husband who had abused her onto the son whom he left for her to raise. Steele and Pollock (1974), who studied sixty families in which "significant" abuse of infants or small children had occurred, stress the heterogeneous nature of this group of parents. They represented "a wide spread of emotional disorders," with only *one* parent diagnosed a sociopath. They came from all socioeconomic and occupational levels, and their IQs ranged from the 70s to 130. They ranged in age from eighteen to forty years, and most of the families were Anglo-Saxon American. Their actions could not be blamed on alcoholism; true alcoholism was found in only one family. One finding stands out as a warning of the long-term effects of severe punishment: "*Without exception* in our study group of abusing parents, there is a history of having been raised in the same style which they have recreated in the pattern of rearing their own children" (Steele and Pollock, 1974, p. 97). This "style" included severe abuse in some, and in all a sense of intense, pervasive, and continuous demand from their parents. They remembered constant parental criticism in their own childhood.

David Gil, who conducted a survey of reported child abuse in the United States in the late 1960s for the then Department of Health, Education and Welfare, concluded that "the approval of a certain measure of physical force as a legitimate and appropriate socializing technique is endemic to American culture." He is convinced that to prevent child abuse would require a major overhaul in how we think about children, how we behave toward them, and major changes in all the institutions that affect the development of children (Gil, 1970, pp. 133–148). In his testimony before the U.S. Senate Subcommittee on Children and Youth, Gil made this recommendation: "Congress ought to outlaw through this bill all forms of physical force used against children in the public domain, in schools, and in child care facilities, under the guise of disciplining them. This form of discipline undermines the human dignity of children. It is nothing but an ancient, cruel ritual which never serves the real educational and developmental needs of children but merely provides ventilation for the frustrations of adults. Being exposed to corporal punishment teaches children that might is right. It results in resentment and fear of their attackers. At best it achieves short-range, externally enforced discipline based on fear but not steady, long-term internalized discipline based on positive identification with caring adults. We know that learning requires positive human relations which are apt to be destroyed by corporal punishment or the ever-present threat of it" (Gil, 1973, p. 9). The bill, referred to as the "Child Abuse Prevention Act," was passed by the Senate in 1973.

The habit of looking at the basis for one's own behavior should be instilled early in childhood, but if that chance has been bypassed or lost, it surely should be encouraged in parent- and teacher-training programs. Teachers probably do no differ from the general population in self-understanding or the lack of it, but their role as educators and their influence on child development present them with a special responsibility to function insightfully. The present trend for schools to have more consultation from mental health workers can only begin to touch the problem.

REFERENCES

Bandura, A., and Walters, R. (1963), *Social Learning and Personality Development.* New York: Holt, Rinehart, & Winston.

Fraiberg, S. H. (1959), *The Magic Years*. New York: Scribner's.

Freud, A. (1974), *Introduction to Psychoanalysis: Lectures for Child Analysts and Teachers*. New York: International Universities Press.

Freud, S. (1930), Civilization and its discontents. *Standard Edition*, 21:59–148. London: Hogarth Press, 1961.

———— (1933), New introductory lectures in psychoanalysis. *Standard Edition*, 22:3–184. London: Hogarth Press, 1964.

Gil, D. S. (1970), *Violence Against Children*. Cambridge, Mass.: Harvard University Press.

———— (1973), Child Abuse Prevention Act. *J. of Clin. Child Psychol.*, 11:7–10.

Hartmann, H. (1960), *Psychoanalysis and Moral Values*. New York: International Universities Press.

———— and Lowenstein, R. (1962), Notes on the superego. *The Psychoanalytic Study of the Child*, 17:42–81. New York: International Universities Press.

Hoffman, M. L. (1970), Moral development. In: *Carmichael's Manual of Child Psychology*, Vol. 2, 3rd ed., ed. P. H. Mussen. New York: Wiley, pp. 261–359.

Kohlberg, L. (1964), Development of moral character and moral ideology. In: *Review of Child Development Research*, Vol. 1, ed. M. L. Hoffman and L. W. Hoffman. New York: Russell Sage, pp. 383–431.

Lampl-de Groot, J. (1962), Ego ideal and superego. *The Psychoanalytic Study of the Child*, 17:94–106. New York: International Universities Press.

Loevinger, J., and Wessler, R. (1970), *Measuring Ego Development*. San Francisco: Jossey-Bass.

Malmquist, C. P. (1968), Conscience development. *The Psychoanalytic Study of the Child*, 23:301–331. New York: International Universities Press.

Steele, B., and Pollock, C. (1974), A psychiatric study of parents who abuse infants and small children. In: *The Battered Child*, ed. R. E. Helfer and C. H. Kempe. Chicago: University of Chicago Press, pp. 89–133.

Stone, L., and Church, J. (1968), *Childhood and Adolescence*. New York: Random House.

Whiting, J., and Child, I. (1953), *Child Training and Personality*. New Haven: Yale University Press.

RECOMMENDED READINGS

S. H. Fraiberg. *The Magic Years*. New York: Scribner's, 1959.

A. Freud. *Introduction to Psychoanalysis: Lectures for Child Analysts and Teachers*. New York: International Universities Press, 1974.

D. S. Gil. *Violence Against Children*. Cambridge, Mass.: Harvard University Press, 1970.

M. L. Hoffman. Moral development. In: *Carmichael's Manual of Child Psychology*, Vol. 2, 3rd ed., ed. P. H. Mussen. New York: Wiley, 1970.

L. Kohlberg. Development of moral character and moral ideology. In: *Review of Child Development Research*, Vol. 1, ed. M. L. Hoffman and L. W. Hoffman. New York: Russell Sage, 1964.

C. P. Malmquist. Conscience development. *The Psychoanalytic Study of the Child*, 23:301–331. New York: International Universities Press, 1968.

L. Stone and J. Church. *Childhood and Adolescence*. New York: Random House, 1968.

3

Discipline: A Piagetian Perspective

Michael Chandler, Ph.D.

The purpose of this chapter is to convey a Piagetian perspective on the disciplining of children. Before acting on this intent, however, two brief but crucial caveats are in order. First, no straightforward recounting of Piaget's position on child discipline is possible, precisely because he has had almost nothing to say on the topic—at least nothing very direct to say. Second, as if this were not obstacle enough, Piaget's theory is primarily an explanatory accounting of children's evolving conceptions of their worlds, and only indirectly a characterization of concrete behaviors and misbehaviors. As such, the theory is poorly suited to the particular action-oriented needs of the disciplinarian in the breach, and its relevance to the general topic of discipline is both somewhat obscure and somewhat oblique.

Despite its only tangential relevance to practical matters of disciplinary tactics, Piagetian theory is very much concerned with those developmental discontinuities which divide children from their parents and which are frequently the occasion for intergenerational discord. For this reason the theory in general, and its application to the topic of moral development in particular, has a clear if indirect bearing on disciplinary matters. What is required, if one wishes to turn Piaget to this purpose, however, is a kind of conceptual rotation which prismatically bends either the theory or the problem in such a way that the two are better conceptually aligned. This chapter attempts such a conceptual realignment by recasting certain traditional issues of discipline into more cognitive-developmental terms. From this altered and more Piagetian perspective, usual text and context are reversed. Rule comprehension becomes figure while rule conformity becomes ground, problems of misconduct are upstaged by problems of morality, and justice becomes more salient than obedience.

If discipline were simply a matter of ensuring behavioral conformity, most or all of these abstractions could be dispensed with and child rearing could be reduced to a science of behavioral engineering. Most parents and caretakers, however, want and expect a great deal more. They intend to rear children who understand the meanings of their rules and disciplinary strategies. They wish to instill a sense of justice as well as to ensure a measure of domestic tranquility, and they wish to bring up children who, in turn, can accomplish these same goals with their own children. For all of these more abstract but more ambitious goals, Piaget's theory has potential relevance.

The pages that follow will, first, locate Piaget's theory of moral development in a broader context of alternative interpretation and, then, specify the delimited areas of this theory applicable to the topic of child discipline. This overview will be followed by a highly skeletal outline of selected aspects of Piaget's developmental account of the moral judgment process, paying special attention to the place of role taking and empathic skill in this process. Finally, attention will be focused on the relationship between moral judgment and moral action, as an intended bridge back to the practical interest that motivates those for whom the development of effective disciplinary methods is more academic.

DISCIPLINE AND MODELS OF MORALITY

One obvious conclusion to be drawn from the chapters of this volume is that discipline is an extremely multi-faceted issue, about which a great diversity of opinion exists. Some of these chapters have focused on how children and adults feel about disciplinary issues, others have centered attention upon disciplinary acts or responses, and still others (the present chapter included) are concerned with how such matters are viewed or understood. Certain of these differences may seem, on the surface, to be only procedural and to center only on tactical questions concerning the best place for research to begin. Lurking behind, and even directing, these surface differences, however, is a series of much more fundamental disagreements about the human condition, about the nature of personal relationships, and about the rules and principles to which they conform. These more general metatheoretical assumptions govern much of what we think about discipline and about how it should be understood and exercised and studied. Some examination of these primitive model assumptions seems essential at the outset. This is particularly the case since the metatheoretical assumptions which underpin Piaget's views on moral development are peculiarly non-American and, thus, much of what he has to say will otherwise seem strange and foreign.

In considering the range of available interpretations regarding moral development, Roger Brown (1965) has distinguished three quite distinct sets of contradictory assumptions, or viewpoints, woven through the fabric of our secularized, Judeo-Christian culture. According to one of these, children are regarded as issued into the world stamped with the moral disfigurement of original sin — a cross-generational stigmata which is thought to be visited upon the offspring even unto the seventh generation. By this view, children are thought to be conceived in sin and lust and to reflect this heritage in their subsequent interaction with others. Society, in this view, is a thin cloak, imperfectly drawn over a body of antisocial impulses and fantasies.

In contrast to this uncharitable, Cotton Mather-like view is a second, which, while equally familiar, contradicts the first at almost every turn. According to this scenario, children enter the world trailing vapors of their divine origin, issued from their maker without spot or blemish. This more Rousseauian view holds that persons, in their feral state, are inherently pure and unsullied, as befits individuals fashioned in the image of their maker. According to this account, corruption is a social disease to which persons are subjected as a consequence of their contacts with civilization. Societies, not the persons who populate them, are the villains of this piece.

A third and more secular alternative is to be found in the *tabula rasa*, or blank slate, assumptions of the English philosopher John Locke. According to this more standoffish interpretation, persons are assumed to be neither inherently good nor bad, but are thought instead to be issued into the world in a state of moral neutrality. What they are to become is thought to be determined after the fact, as the hand of experience writes on them for better or for worse.

Lest you are misled into thinking that these quaint historical assumptions have little relevance to modern psychology, let me quickly stress that each of these seemingly old-fashioned, metatheoretical postures has its contemporary expression in current brands of social-science theory and research. The doctrine of original sin is still very much alive and would appear to shape the essential features of id-oriented and impulse-bedecked psychoanalytic and psychodynamic theories. The Lockean assumptions of moral neutrality have filtered down, essentially unchanged, into contemporary behavioral theories that characterize socialization as a kind of experiential summary. Finally, the notion of innate purity has its more modern expression in the theories of Piaget and Kohlberg, which turn the problem on its head and see morality, not as innately given, but as the almost inevitable consequence to which persons are led by the force of their own normative development.

Having outlined a range of equally available metatheoretical postures that one might assume about the natural relationship of persons to some moral order, let me now be somewhat less survey oriented and evenhanded as I attempt to both detail and advocate what Piaget's position is on these matters and, in the process, to suggest the important implications of these views for the study and understanding of discipline. First, let me remind the reader where I think most of us are coming from. According to a popular, man-on-the-street view of morality, behavior is understood as the algebraic outcome of two forces, the lust of the flesh (needs, impulses) on the one hand, and the anticipation of guilt or punishment on the other (Kohlberg, 1971). Morality or moral learning is seen in this commonsense view as fundamentally emotional or irrational and is thought to represent successful resistance to temptation based on mechanisms of guilt, habit, identification, or defense. Both children and adults are seen to operate in terms of a kind of neo-Malthusian principle (Burke, 1972), according to which lax habits are expected to proliferate insofar as conditions make indulgences possible. Social organization in general and discipline in particular are seen, from this man-on-the-street perspective, as important coercive checks on less desirable natural tendencies (Hogan and Dickstein, 1972). The Piagetian perspective openly rejects this common moral metaphor of intrapsychic conflict and individual self-control as a restatement of the shopworn and misleading mind-body dichotomy that has divided psychology (Wilden, 1975). In this view, attempts to characterize morality as a conflict between the flesh and the spirit, or between an irrational id and an equally irrational, but socialized, superego are regarded as seriously misleading (Kohlberg, 1971). Children are seen instead as the products of a long evolutionary history of group living, are thought to be inherently culture bearing, intrinsically rule following, and naturally predisposed toward socialization (Hogan, 1975; Waddington, 1967). As organized systems in open relation to environmental information, regulation does not imply, in this view, internal adjustments or self-regulation, but rather, an informed adaptation. As in any valid cybernetic system, regulatory crises are seen as responses to ambiguities or loss of feedback from the environment rather than as failures in self-control (Kohlberg, 1971).

It is perhaps noteworthy in this regard that parents of very young infants commonly hold views similar to these. They deal with personally unpleasant or disruptive behavior on the part of their children as naturally occurring regulatory crises and rarely resort to punitive or coercive disciplinary strategies. Hoffman (1975), for example, reports that less than 5 percent of the interactions between parents and their very young infants could be fairly characterized as disciplinary. Two years later, however, most parents have exchanged their earlier systems-oriented views for a set of much more dualistic assumptions about internal problems in self-control, and the proportion of their interactions with their children that are disciplinary in character typically exceeds 50 percent. Having rejected a view of children as inherently at war within themselves or with their society, Piaget's theory effectively redefines the context of socialization and casts it into much less combative terms. While this represents a radical break with American psychological tradition, its effect is only to neutralize, not eliminate, the necessary process of socialization. Piaget, like those theorists whose views he rejects, must provide an accounting of the socialization process. For Piaget much, but not all, of this effort is contained in his theory of moral development.

RULE LEARNING vs. MORAL DEVELOPMENT

Although it might seem, to you and me, intuitively obvious that the first minimal requirement for rule-observant behavior is knowledge of the rules (Hogan, 1975), this easy assumption has not been widely maintained in American psychology. As Kohlberg (1971) has pointed out, behavioristic psychology has focused its attention on "learning" rather than "knowing" and social development is understood as conformity to, rather than knowledge of, societal expectation. Discipline, in the context of American psychology, is equated with training strategies, the effectiveness of which is assumed to rest entirely upon an adequate accounting of how response-learning proceeds and is retained. For the most part, these accounts have incorporated familiar assumptions about punishment and reward, modeling and identification, extinction and generalization. Beyond these easy rules of thumb, little is commonly added to accounts of moral

education that would not also apply equally to paper-
training your dog. Other than certain Piagetian inspired
studies of moral development, little or no attention has
been given to the possibility that not all rules and not all
children are of the same order of complexity. The process
of learning truths has been assumed to be the same as the
process of learning lies or illusions, and the teaching of
moral systems has been thought identical to the process
involved in learning social dance steps (Kohlberg, 1971,
pp. 151–152.).

In sharp contrast to these views, Piaget has argued
that children do not simply adapt to social customs and
conventions, but actively structure and transform what
is socially given in ways that are consistent with their
momentary level of cognitive development. Moral development, in this sense, is seen to involve more than the
simple rank-and-file accumulation of social habits; it is
thought instead to represent the orderly transformation
of cognitive structures in interaction with social experience (Turiel, 1975). The eventual product of these developmental processes is not simply a known catalog of the
basic moral rules or conventions of society, but an operative system capable of autonomously generating a principled and coherent behavioral code.

STAGES IN MORAL DEVELOPMENT
AND DISCIPLINARY STRATEGIES

Readers acquainted with the broad outlines of Piaget's theory are likely to be most familiar with the step-
wise sequence of discrete stages which he feels segment
the process of general cognitive development. These stage
descriptions, while not necessarily the most novel aspects
of Piaget's work, are certainly the best remembered and
often serve as touchstones for persons otherwise uncom-

fortable with the unfamiliar turf of his genetic epistemology. For the reader familiar with this view who has been either patiently or impatiently waiting for this discussion to get down to the real issue of one stage versus the next, it is important to point out that Piaget has never been fully convinced that matters of moral development shape themselves into a discrete-stage sequence as do other matters of cognitive development (Piaget, 1932). Although some interpreters have viewed this as resulting from the early place of *The Moral Judgment of the Child* in the chronology of his writings, there remains real doubt whether Piaget ever intended to discuss moral issues in the same segmented fashion that he approached more logically based matters of cognitive development (Piaget, 1970).

Quite apart from the question of whether matters of moral judgment shape themselves into a logically implicative sequence of hierarchically embedded stages, Piaget, nevertheless, has been impressed that the manner in which children think about moral issues does change dramatically with advancing intellectual development.

> [Within his theory] the most important aspect of this development lies in advances from an earlier stage where social relations are . . . seen to be characterized by heteronomy or external constraint, where rules are interpreted as sacred, to a more autonomous state where social relations are characterized by cooperation and an attitude of mutual respect, and where rules are accepted as binding by mutual agreement rather than immutably given by authority [Graham, 1972, p. 192].

Depending on where and how one reads Piaget, these two periods can be supplemented by an earlier mode of motor rules and regularities and a later formal operational period of principle-oriented, generative moral structures. Kohlberg (1963) and others have further expanded and crystalized these changes into more or less explicit stages of moral development.

At least for present purposes, the central thing to keep in mind about these alternatives and developmentally dependent strategies for regarding moral issues is that, for Piaget, each reflects a unique and qualitatively different construction of the world, and that events can be understood at or below one's current operative level, but not above. It is the special relevance of this feature of the moral-development process which has the most direct bearing on disciplinary strategies.

CHILDREN'S AND SOCIALIZING AGENTS' MORAL DEVELOPMENT

If, as the work of Turiel (1966, 1969) and others has demonstrated, children are sharply limited in their ability to comprehend, accommodate to, comply with, or otherwise appreciate moral injunctions couched at developmental levels substantially beyond their own, then special problems are set for disciplinarians whose level of moral maturity greatly exceeds that of the child they seek to influence and control. One may not formulate, of course, a moral system or a disciplinary strategy more complicated than oneself; the level of moral development achieved by a particular parent or disciplinarian necessarily sets upper limits on the kind of justice that he or she may mete out. The lower bound of the moral-development strategy chosen, however, is often more relevant and more negotiable. On the one hand, parents must live with the fact that they are accountable for their own actions and feel a responsibility to behave toward their children in accordance with whatever code of conduct they set for themselves. Many parents, for example, refuse to employ corporal punishment, not because they suspect it is necessarily inefficient, but because such physical violence against children violates their own sense of justice. Statements such as "This is going to hurt me more than it hurts you" are therefore sometimes a comment on the fact that certain disciplinary actions grate upon, or violate, the speaker's sense of preferred conduct.

In addition to the attempt to identify a disciplinary strategy consistent with their own morality, many parents, sensitive to developmental differences in moral maturity, seek to employ tactics which are capable of being understood, and regarded as just by their children, as well as by themselves. Satisfying this dual criteria becomes increasingly difficult when the moral-development levels of parent and child are most divergent: that is, when the most stages separate the developmental levels of parent and child. What children of different ages regard as just and equitable punishment varies, as Piaget (1932) has shown, across an extremely broad range. Preschool children commonly see punishment as retaliatory; for them, punishments need, in no sense, fit the crime. Somewhat older children reinvent the ancient law of *lex talionis* and see an eye for an eye as the most fitting form of punishment. Preadolescent children look for justice in fixed penalties for fixed crime and support no tempering of law in response to extenuating circumstances. Only in adolescence, according to Piaget, do children routinely come to adopt a view of distributive justice in which punishments are intended to repair the offense which occasioned them.

Parents who insist on modes of discipline which go well beyond their children's own assumptions about just deserts are unlikely to be seen by them as fair or equitable, and the moral lesson intended may be entirely lost. Disciplinary tactics less mature than those spontaneously held by a child are likely to seem to them capricious and arbitrary and vengeful. To complicate matters still further, a part of each parent's responsibility is to lead and instruct his or her children in modes of morality by holding them to progressively more mature standards. In brief a parent risks being misunderstood if he or she adopts disciplinary strategies either too far above or below the developmental level of the child. More complicated still is the fact that a disciplinary strategy which is easily understood is comforting, but not growth inducing. Even a Goldilocks strategy of "just right" is not just right if the child is to be effectively lured to his or her next developmental level.

Effective discipline, viewed from this Piagetian perspective, requires an extremely sensitive and continuously contemporized reading of the child's developmental level of moral maturity. By this explanatory model, children who are held to systems of morality that they cannot conceptually grasp are doomed to mistakes of ignorance and fall into errors of their ways in a manner comparable to that of an adult who violates rules of bridge which have not yet been entirely grasped. Conversely, the child who is held to some moral code less lofty than his or her own best understanding of morality feels unfairly and arbitrarily dealt with. This already complex monitoring process is further complicated by the fact that certain matters of conduct, concerned with societal customs and conventions, appear to follow a developmental sequence which differs from issues of morality and ethicality per se (Turiel, 1975). Whether one should tip one's hat to or open doors for a lady is not, it would appear, a matter of the same order as whether one should steal. There is also evidence (Hogan, 1975) to suggest that a child's level of moral maturity varies with the culturally specific content of the moral issues at hand and with whether the particular values proposed agree with the child's own. "Thou shalt honor thy father and thy mother" is probably a dictate of the same order as "thou shalt not fink on a friend." Children who live in a complex multilayered culture consequently often experience contradictory and incompatible rules of the same logical order.

In the face of this complexity and given the special relevance of developmental dimensions (of which most parents are only vaguely or intuitively aware), it is not surprising that children are often held to moral principles which they have no reasonable prospect of understanding. Similarly, children are frequently misjudged or accused of moral lapses that have no meaning in their own developmentally determined code of morality. The most extreme examples of such misperceptions are found in samples of child-abusing parents (Sameroff and Chandler, 1975) who often attribute malevolence, vindictiveness, and purposeful rule violations to their infant children. Similar, but less radical, misjudgments are commonplace occurrences on the part of parents and educators who offer overly abstract and principle-oriented interpretations of social issues to early-school-age children. The opposite side of this same coin occurs whenever adults seriously underestimate or undershoot the ethical achievements of young persons under their moral direction. If one can analogize from Kohlberg's (1969) finding on the interpretation of dreams (the potential negative impact of urging on children's beliefs that are less cognitively mature than their own), then the negative consequences of holding persons to developmentally inferior moral standards could be quite far-reaching. This research suggests that holding a child to an interpretation of events less developmentally complex than his or her own has a kind of leveling effect that reduces all of one's judgments to the lowest common denominator. Taken to an extreme, this

suggests that persons tend to apply standards of morality
equal to that of the most developmentally inferior level
to which they are held accountable.

Whereas most of the difficulties in cross-generational moral interactions would appear to occur as a result of
failures to detect real differences in the moral codes of different age groups, other potential problems arise precisely because such differences are fairly recognized and tak-
en into account. It's another "damned if you do, damned
if you don't" situation. The problem in this case arises
from the fact that adults who hold persons of different
ages to different sets of moral principles exercise, in so doing, a double or even hypocritical standard, The research
of Bryan (1975) and others strongly suggests that parents
caught in repeated hypocrisies lose their effectiveness as
social reinforcers in their children's eyes. The key word
here, however, is *caught*. Both here and elsewhere much
that is central in the course of moral development is seen
by Piagetian theorists to rest on the only gradually ma-
turing ability to formulate nonegocentric, socially decen-
tered judgments about others.

SOCIAL ROLE TAKING, MORAL DEVELOPMENT, AND MORAL TRAINING

The resolution of conflicting interpersonal claims is
seen by Piaget to hinge on how these claims are antici-
pated and understood. The underlying skill, upon which
success in such situations rests, is what Piaget (1970) has
characterized as "social decentration"—that is, the ability
to simultaneously consider and coordinate multiple dimensions of a multidimensional problem and to arrive at
inferential conclusions which reflect this capacity. Moral
judgment, for Piaget, is essentially the operation of such
social-decentering or social-perspective-taking skills in a
moral context. In this view the relationship of role taking

and moral development is not, as is sometimes suggested, one of simple empirical covariation of cause and effect, but is rather a case of special application. Although Kohlberg (1969) and Selman (1971) have argued the evidence somewhat differently and suggest that role taking is a necessary, but not sufficient, condition for sophisticated moral judgments, there appears to be a consensus among concerned scholars that training in role-taking skills is the surest and most defensible route to the training of moral-judgment skills (Chandler, 1975). Several lines of research support this conclusion. The research of Staub (1975) on helping behavior; the attempts at moral education undertaken by Kohlberg and his colleagues (1970); Turiel's (1969) research on the training of moral judgments; and the author's own intervention efforts with delinquent and antisocial children (Chandler, 1973; Chandler et al., 1973) — all support the conclusion that training in role-taking skills serves to increase the complexity of moral reasoning, helping behavior, concern for others, and prosocial conduct. In this context, the repeated demonstrations by Hoffman (1970) that parenting styles emphasizing the consequences of a child's behavior on others (induction) increase prosocial behavior, can be seen as a kind of home-based training in social role taking.

In addition to these pragmatic, utilitarian arguments for the efficacy of role-taking training as a technique for advancing moral development, Kohlberg urges the point on more ethical grounds. According to this view, Kohlberg maintains "that the stimulation of development is the only ethically acceptable form of moral education" (Kohlberg, 1971, p. 153) in which a social scientist can engage, because to do otherwise would be to presume to champion particular moral contents. Attempts at moral education that seek to develop the organizational structures by which one analyzes, interprets, and makes decisions about social problems avoid the difficulty associated with the advocacy of a particular brand of morality. It is, I believe, worth considering that parents as well as social scientists adopt this kind of ethical stance. In a world in which our children rarely live out their lives in a moral context similar to that of their parents, the direct advocacy of parental values has become less of an unremittingly good thing.

MORAL THOUGHT AND MORAL BEHAVIOR

Most of what has been said so far has concerned issues of moral thought — that is, how children think about moral issues and how we, as adults responsible for their upbringing, might best deal with these considerations. What has been left largely unsaid up to this point is the nature of the relationship between moral judgment and actions.

The routine, knee-jerk criticism of cognitive theories such as Piaget's is that they leave the audience hopelessly lost in thought. While it might be generally argued that if you must be lost, in thought is not such a bad place to be lost, a volume such as this, devoted to the practical considerations of discipline and training, is probably not the place to open that argument. This essay will conclude, therefore, by addressing the nature of this relationship between thought and behavior as it is expressed in Piaget's theory.

First, it is important to recognize that the word *moral* is not a proper modifier of the word behavior. Behavior as such is neither moral nor immoral. What we usually have in mind when loosely speaking of moral behavior is something more akin to behavioral conformity or adherence to some set of rules or laws or expectations. Second, it must be recognized that knowledge or understanding of moral rules or principles bears with it no obligation to employ these principles in the service of justice. Complex knowledge of rules and regulations are in fact sometimes the instrument which makes rule violation possible. Despite these disclaimers, however, moral conceptualizations and the societal rules and expectations which they generate are explicitly designed to arbitrate the conflicting interests and actions of different individuals. Specific forms of moral action commonly presuppose specific forms of moral thought as prerequisitive. As such these moral values and principles are assumed to mediate prosocial behavior. In addressing this point, Piaget asks, "Is man merely a maker of phrases that have no relation to his real actions, or is the need to formulate part of his very being?" (Piaget, 1932, p. 109). Kohlberg, in this same context, has criticized psychology as operating as though the relation of belief to action is independent of the general cognitive adequacy of the belief (Kohlberg, 1971). In support of his confidence in the behavioral efficacy of belief, he cites research which demonstrates that whereas younger children cheat more when the probability of getting caught is reduced (for example, when an honor system is being employed), it is precisely under such circumstances that older and more principled children cheat the least.

With or without such evidence, Piaget and moral theorists like him reflect in their work the kind of optimistic commitment voiced centuries ago by Socrates: "Virtue is knowledge of the good. He who knows the good chooses the good." That may, in this post-Watergate era, seem too naïve for your taste, but then we were not all involved in the Watergate conspiracy.

REFERENCES

Brown, R. (1965), *Social Psychology*. New York: The Free Press.

Bryan, J. H. (1975), You will be well advised to watch what we do instead of what we say. In: *Moral Development: Current Theory and Research*, ed. D. J. DePalma and J. M. Foley. Hillside, N.J.: Lawrence Erlbaum, pp. 95–111.

Burke, K. (1972), *Dramatism and Development*. Worcester, Mass.: Clark University Press/Barre, 1972.

Chandler, M. J. (1973), Egocentrism and antisocial behavior: The assessment and training of social perspective-taking skills. *Dev. Psychol.*, 9(3):326–332.

———— (1975), Role Taking and Moral Development. Paper presented at the 1975 Eastern Psychological Association, April 3–5, New York, New York.

———— Greenspan, S., and Barenboim, C. (1973), Judgments of intentionality in response to videotaped and verbally presented moral dilemmas: The medium is the message. *Child Development*, 44:315–320.

Graham, D. (1972), *Moral Learning and Development: Theory and Research*. New York: Wiley.

Hoffman, M. L. (1970), Moral Development. In: *Carmichael's Handbook of Child Psychology*, Vol. 2, ed. P. H. Mussen. New York: Wiley.

———— (1975), Moral internalization, parental power, and the nature of parent-child interaction. *Developmental Psychology*, 2(2):228–239.

Hogan, R. (1975), Moral development and the structure of personality. In: *Moral Development: Current Theory and Research*, ed. D. J. DePalma and J. M. Foley. Hillside, N.J.: Lawrence Erlbaum.

———— and Dickstein, E. (1972), A measure of moral values. *Journal of Consult. and Clin. Psychol.*, 39:210–214.

Kohlberg, L. (1963), Moral development and identification. In: *Child Psychology: The 62nd Yearbook of the National Society for the Study of Education*, ed. H. Stevenson. Chicago: University of Chicago Press, pp. 277–332.

———— (1969), Stage and sequence: The cognitive-developmental approach to socialization. In: *Handbook of Socialization Theory and Research*, ed. D. Goslin. New York: Rand McNally, pp. 347–380.

———— (1970), Education for justice: A modern statement of the Platonic view. In: *Moral Education: Five Lectures*, ed. N. F. Sizer and P. R. Sizer. Cambridge, Mass.: Harvard University Press, pp. 57–83.

———— (1971), From is to ought: How to commit the natural fallacy and get away with it in the study of moral development. In: *Cognitive Development and Epistemology*, ed. T. Mischel. New York: Academic Press.

Piaget, J. (1932), *The Moral Judgment of the Child*. London: Kegan Paul.

———— (1970), Piaget's theory. In: *Carmichael's Manual of Child Psychology*, Vol. 1, ed. P. H. Mussen. New York: Wiley, pp. 703–732.

Sameroff, A. J., and Chandler, M. J. (1975), Reproductive risk and the continuum of caretaking casualty. In: *Review of Child Development Research*, Vol. 4, ed. F. D. Horowitz. Chicago: University of Chicago Press, pp. 187–244.

Selman, R. (1971), The relation of role-taking to moral judgment. *Child Development*, 42:79–91.

Staub, E. (1975), To rear a prosocial child: Reasoning, learning by doing, and learning to teach others. In: *Moral Development: Current Theory and Research*, ed. D. J. DePalma and J. M. Foley. Hillside, N.J.: Lawrence Erlbaum, pp. 113–135.

Turiel, E. (1966), An experimental test of the sequentiality of developmental stages in the child's moral judgments. *J. of Personality and Soc. Psychol.*, 3(6):611–618.

———— (1969), Developmental processes in children's moral thinking. In: *Trends and Issues in Developmental Psychology*, ed. P. Mussen, J. Langer, and M. Covington. New York: Holt, Rinehart, & Winston, pp. 92–133.

———— (1975), The development of social concepts: Mores, customs, and conventions. In: *Moral Development: Current Theory and Research*, ed. D. J. DePalma and J. M. Foley. Hillside, N.J.: Lawrence Erlbaum, pp. 7–37.

Waddington, C. H. (1967), *The Ethical Animal*. Chicago: University of Chicago Press.

Wilden, A. (1975), Piaget and the structure as law and order.
    In: *Structure and Transformation: Developmental and
    Historical Aspects*, ed. K. F. Riegel and G. C. Rosenwald.
    New York: Wiley, pp. 83–117.

4

The Rational-Emotive Point of View of Discipline

Virginia Waters, Ph.D.

Within the rational-emotive therapy framework, discipline is viewed as an ongoing process, the purpose of which is to help children think independently and learn to control their own behavior. In expanding upon this orientation, I shall first describe the rational-emotive theoretical and therapeutic framework and its application to children and youth and then explain how discipline is conceptualized and practiced within this framework.

INTRODUCTION TO RATIONAL-EMOTIVE THERAPY

History and Development

Rational-emotive therapy is a cognitive-behavioral approach to helping people understand and solve their problems. RET, as the approach is called, was developed by Albert Ellis in the 1950s and is based on the assumption that individuals create their own disturbances by making unrealistic demands on themselves and others and by adhering to irrational systems of beliefs. The goal of RET is to help people learn how to lead non-self-defeating, happier lives by teaching them to cope better with themselves, with others, and with their environments (Ellis, 1957, 1962a, 1962b). This is achieved through instructing individuals in how to examine their thoughts and beliefs critically, and how to challenge self-defeating beliefs in order to help develop a more tolerant, accepting, and humanistic philosophy of life. In short, the goal of RET is to help people to think better, not just to feel better or to give up their symptoms (Ellis, 1973c).

Ellis originated RET in the 1950s after having been trained as a psychoanalyst and having practiced psychoanalysis, psychoanalytically oriented therapies, and various other methods, all of which he found to be largely ineffective (Ellis, 1974). He observed that although clients in psychoanalysis were able to achieve insights into their disturbance, their behaviors and inappropriate emotions were left untouched. In addition, Ellis found psychoanalysis to be too slow, too past oriented, too passive, and not useful to clients in enabling them to see how they continued to upset themselves, as well as how they might learn to modify their own emotional upset. As a result of observing these psychoanalytic deficiencies, Ellis developed his own therapeutic theory and technique — one that stresses the interdependence of thinking, feeling, and behaving and that advocates teaching individuals rational thinking skills in order to promote appropriate as opposed to inappropriate emotions. Hence, the name, rational-emotive therapy.

Basic Assumptions of Rational-Emotive Therapy

RET is based upon a number of fundamental assumptions that Ellis maintains are essential to an understanding of human disturbance and its treatment.
1. *The A, B, C theory of emotional disturbance.* People

tend to disturb themselves as the result of faulty evaluations of themselves, of others, and of the world. In other words, feelings are precipitated by beliefs and thoughts, and not by events or the actions of others. In a nutshell: "We feel the way we think." RET promotes an *A, B, C* theory of emotional healthfulness and disturbance. The *A* of the formulation represents the activating event or situation that, when viewed through *B*, one's belief system, leads to *C*, or the emotional consequences experienced as unpleasant. *B* or beliefs may be either rational or irrational. Rational beliefs are those that maximize pleasure, minimize pain, and are empirically observable, while irrational beliefs are those that decrease pleasure, increase pain, and are not empirically observable. According to this system, it is not the activating event or the *A* that leads to *C*, the emotional consequence, for if this were true we would all react identically to the same situation. It is what one believes about the event that leads to the panic, anxiety, and depression one might feel at *C*.

To illustrate how this formulation works in practice, I offer the following examples which are also schematized in Figures 1 and 2. Two young children playing by the seashore are knocked down by a wave. One child may be very upset and run to mother while the other may be delighted and wait eagerly for another wave. The action of the environment on each child was identical but the emotional response and accompanying behavior differed significantly. The reasons for these differences can be understood in terms of each child's attitude toward or assessment of what happened (Young, 1974).

Suppose a parent disciplines two fighting siblings by sending each to his own room. One child might be happy because he wished some time to himself to construct his new model plane. The other child might be unhappy because he wanted to go outside and play with his friends.

Figure 1

	A Activating Event	B Irrational or Rational Belief	C Emotional Consequence	Behavioral Reaction
Child 1	A wave knocks down children at play in the ocean	"I can't stand to be frightened! This is awful!"	Fear	Runs to mother, stays out of water
Child 2		"What fun! I really like this!"	Excitement	Stays in the water

The punishment was the same, but the children's different *attitudes* about it resulted in two different reactions (Ellis, 1962b, 1971).

2. *Rational and irrational beliefs.* "RET emphasizes that people have both rational and irrational values and behaviors. It can be assumed that almost all humans have the basic goals of wanting to survive, to be relatively happy, to get along with members of their social group, and to relate intimately to a few members of this group. Once these basic values are assumed, anything that aids them is rational or appropriate, and anything that sabotages them is inappropriate" (Ellis, 1974, p. 195).

It would seem that most individuals adhere to a similar set of irrational beliefs, and it is the function of the therapist to help the client to identify his or her particular set of self-defeating beliefs and challenge and dispute them.

The main irrational ideas that most people seem to subscribe to in order to manufacture their own states of panic, self-blame, and self-doubt appear to be:

1. The idea that it is a dire necessity for an adult to be loved or approved by virtually every signifi-

Figure 2

A Activating Event	B Irrational or Rational Belief	C Emotional Consequence	Behavioral Reaction
Child 1	"It's unfair! I wanted to go out and play. I can't stand not getting what I want!"	Anger Resentment	Sulks, slams door to his room
Mother sends fighting siblings			
Child 2 to their rooms	"It's a pain to be punished, but this gives me a chance to work on my model. I'll make the best of it."	Mild irritation, resignation	Goes to room and becomes absorbed in working on model

cant person in his community.

2. The idea that one should be thoroughly competent, adequate, and achieving in all possible respects if one is to consider oneself worthwhile.

3. The idea that human happiness is externally caused and that people have little or no ability to control their sorrows or disturbances.

4. The idea that one's past history is an all-important determinant of one's present behavior and that because something once strongly affected one's life, it should indefinitely have a similar effect.

5. The idea that there is invariably a right, precise, and perfect solution to human problems and that it is catastrophic if this perfect solution is not found.

6. The idea that if something is or may be dangerous or fearsome one should be terribly concerned
about it and should keep dwelling on the possibility of its occurring.

The main irrational ideas that men and women seem
to endorse in order to create their own states of
anger, moralizing, and low frustration tolerance are
these:

1. The idea that certain people are bad, wicked, or
villainous and that they should be severely
blamed and punished for their villainy.
2. The idea that it is awful and catastrophic when
things are not the way one would very much like
them to be.
3. The idea that it is easier to avoid than to face certain life difficulties and self-responsibilities.
4. The idea that one should become quite upset over
other people's problems and disturbances (Ellis,
1973b, p. 152).

3. *Appropriate and inappropriate emotions.* RET makes
a distinction between appropriate and inappropriate
emotions. Appropriate emotions, whether positive or
negative, are viewed as reactions realistic to one's situation, that are not self-defeating; whereas inappropriate
emotions tend to be overreactions to a situation and to be
self-defeating.

RET consequently designates certain negative
emotions — such as sorrow, regret, irritation and annoyance — as appropriate when individuals are faced
with obnoxious stimuli, since these emotions motivate them to remove or change these stimuli; and it
designates certain emotions — such as anxiety, depression, feelings of worthlessness, and hostility — as

inappropriate, since such emotions encourage people to become obsessed with but not do anything effective to change obnoxious stimuli [Ellis, 1974, p. 195].

Anger, for instance, is designated as an inappropriate emotion because it usually includes the grandiose demand that others *must* not behave in ways which displease us. Ellis notes that "feeling and expressing rage almost always leads to poor results in terms of personal happiness and getting along with others, and that feeling angry without expressing it rips up one's own guts and leads to distinct harm. The most elegant solution to the problem is to radically change one's views about how others *should* behave, and thereby get rid of the hostility entirely" (Ellis, 1974, p. 197). In short, RET advocates maintain that learning to prevent self-destructive emotions, such as anger and hostility, is the best solution and that the expression of appropriate emotions, such as irritability and annoyance when thwarted, is appropriate and health inducing.

4. *Biosocial theory of personality development.* Ellis assumes that man is a biosocial animal, the product of an interaction between innate predispositions and experiential learning (Ellis, 1974, p. 194). Consequently people are born with a tendency to think and behave both rationally and irrationally; however, it would seem that irrational thought is more often and more vigorously reinforced by the culture and, subsequently, perpetuated by individual self-conditioning. Ellis also believes that human beings have a natural tendency to easily upset themselves.

5. *Acceptance and worth.* Because individuals are composed of a complex matrix of traits and characteristics, it is pointless, self-defeating, and scientifically unsound to rate anyone globally as either good or bad, either worth-

while or worthless. It is possible, however, to rate individual traits and characteristics (Ellis, 1974, p. 197). For instance, one might say to a child, "You behaved inconsiderately to your sister this morning, and that sort of behavior is unacceptable to me." This would be an instance of rating the specific behavior in a single situation, as opposed to saying "You are inconsiderate and unacceptable to me," which implies that the child is always, under all conditions, in all situations, inconsiderate. Rather than using global ratings, individuals are encouraged to accept themselves unconditionally (negative traits and all) simply because they are alive, and refrain from self-blame and "self-downing" in every situation. This is not to say that people are not encouraged to improve weak or poor traits, but rather that they accept themselves while attempting to improve these traits.

6. *Demandingness.* A major source of human disturbance is making demands on oneself and others. Ellis defines "practically all emotional disturbance as being the product of demanding as opposed to desiring" (Ellis, 1974, p. 196). People who dictate or insist that they themselves perform in a certain way or that others conform to their wishes are headed for emotional upset. The words *should, ought,* and *must* signal a demand and had best be eliminated from use. For example, the child who demands that he absolutely must have a cookie before dinner will be far more upset if his mother denies his demand than will a child who merely prefers to have a cookie, but realizes that he doesn't have to have it.

7. *Awfulizing.* Individuals tend to create their own disturbance by "catastrophizing" the severity of their situation. Those who "awfulize" by cognitively augmenting the ramifications of a situation are on the road to emotional disturbance. An individual who maintains that it is awful and intolerable that he cannot have what he be-

lieves he must is creating more discomfort for himself than he need experience by making his reaction to his original problem of deprivation an additional problem. It is bad enough to suffer from deprivation, but making that suffering an additional problem is a needless dose of double trouble.

8. *Individual choice to change.* Because individuals have the ability to control their emotions by controlling their thinking, they can, to a large extent, choose how they are going to feel and can learn to think more rationally and thereby lead less self-defeating lives. The best ways an individual can work on changing his irrationality are: (1) cognitively, by actively challenging and disputing his irrational beliefs, and (2) behaviorally, by changing and modifying his self-defeating behaviors. For example, a woman who believes she is unattractive and therefore undesirable, and as a result isolates herself from social situations, might be given the therapeutic homework assignment of (1) cognitively challenging the idea that it would be awful if she were unattractive and were rejected as a result and (2) behaviorally approaching two men during the following week in order to: (a) test the hypothesis that she is ugly and undesirable, (b) if she is rejected, give her an opportunity to see that it isn't the end of the world, and (c) to help her change the behavior of isolating herself from others that is contributing to the perpetuation of the irrational belief that she is unattractive.

9. *A mentally healthy individual.* A person displaying mental health as opposed to neurotic tendencies has a minimum of hostility ("blaming others and the world around him," Ellis, 1973b, p. 147) and anxiety (self-downing), and can unconditionally accept himself as a fallible human being. "Several additional positive goals of mental health are implicit or explict in the teachings of

RET: (1) self-interest; (2) self-direction; (3) tolerance; (4) acceptance of uncertainty; (5) flexibility; (6) scientific thinking; (7) commitment; and (8) risk taking" (Ellis, 1973b).

THE RELEVANCE OF RET TO CHILDREN

Although RET was originally designed to deal with adult emotional disturbance, its basic tenets are easily and effectively applied to the management of children (Ellis et al., 1975; Hauck, 1973; Knaus, 1974). RET is based on an educational model and advocates teaching the principles of emotional upset and health to all children and adults as a means of providing them with a coping strategy capable of minimizing, if not of preventing, present and future disturbance. It also follows that if children do indeed have a natural tendency to think both rationally and irrationally and to upset themselves easily, they could benefit from learning to practice rational thinking at an early age. This would enable them to avoid years spent disturbing themselves as the result of continued irrational thinking. Parents could also benefit from an understanding of the principles of RET. If their goal is to raise a healthy, happy, clear-thinking child, rather than an anxious, whining, crooked-thinking neurotic, they had better try to provide that child with good models of rational living by practicing it themselves, as well as by instructing their children in how to lead non-self-defeating lives.

Since the creation of RET in the 1950s, one of the major additions to it has been the development of techniques and procedures specifically designed to help children grow up to be healthy adults (Ellis et al., 1975). The Living School, which was started by the Institute for Advanced Study in Rational Psychotherapy in 1968, was designed to infuse the principles of emotional education and rational living into the academic curriculum (Knaus, 1974). In addition, rational–emotive education (REE), the educational arm of RET, advocates the active-directive instruction of the principles of emotional education to all school children and youth. REE has been expanding into all areas of the country and through all areas of the curriculum as well (Daly, 1971; Ellis, 1969, 1971, 1973a). Currently the REE consultation service is providing training for teachers who wish to become more proficient consumers and communicators of RET problem-solving skills.

The Roots of Emotional Disturbance: How to Raise a Neurotic

Since it could be agreed that the goal of most parents is to raise a nonneurotic child, it might be helpful at this point to examine the roots of emotional disturbance and the characteristics that distinguish neurotic from nonneurotic behavior. A neurotic might be described as an individual who persists in embracing childish ideas (Ellis, 1975). In addition neurotics tend to display an overabundance of: (1) feelings of inadequacy, (2) guilt and self-blame, (3) hostility and resentment, (4) ingratiation, (5) ineffectiveness, (6) self-deceit and lack of realism, (7) rigidity and compulsiveness, (8) shyness and withdrawal, (9) psychosomatic symptoms, (10) crackpotism and bizarreness, (11) depression, (12) over-excitability, (13) inertia and lack of direction, (14) overambitiousness and compulsive striving, and (15) self-downing and punishment.

Ellis maintains that neurotic disturbance results from three main influences: (1) our inborn tendencies to think, feel, and act in certain ways, (2) the environmental and cultural circumstances in which we are reared, and (3) the ways we choose to act or condition ourselves to the things we experience. The mechanisms for neuroticism and emotional disturbance are acquired in childhood, when irrational beliefs and attitudes are assimilated into one's belief system. These unrealistic beliefs, usually regarding what life conditions must or must not exist in order for us to be happy, are a major cause of emotional misery (Ellis, 1975).

One way that a parent can be sure to raise a neurotic is to continue to adhere to and act in accordance with these irrational beliefs, thus reinforcing them in their children as well. Because early self-concept formation tends to depend on the attitudes of significant others in one's life, it is important for adults to examine what attitudinal messages they are conveying to their children. If a parent or teacher blames a child, that child will tend to blame himself. If they generally accept the child, the child will be more likely to accept himself. If they convey to the child that it is awful to fail or make a mistake, the child will tend to rate himself as a failure if he is not perfect. Although early learnings about self are important in creating later patterns, it is never too late to change self-concept for better or worse.

More commonly, however, children are raised in an atmosphere of criticism in which they are taught to equate the negative reaction to misdeed (e.g., making a mess) with a negative appraisal of the self (e.g., "I am a bad person"). If children are consistently told that they are naughty or bad when they perform certain acts or exhibit certain behaviors and that they will not be loved if this continues, they will incorporate these ideas into their belief system, where they will be the stimuli to future upsets. Because children overgeneralize they readily accept the propositions that they must earn a good self-concept through good works and that if they fail in their endeavors to do good they truly are unacceptable to anyone and this is catastrophic. This manner of thinking inevitably stimulates the development of profound feelings of inadequacy and resentment as well as other elements of emotional maladjustment.

On the other hand, in order to raise a healthy, happy child, parents are encouraged to help their children give up their irrational thinking; to learn to accept unfortunate circumstances, rather than awfulize and catastrophize about them; to learn how to solve problems, rather than bemoan them; to learn to accept themselves and conditions they cannot change fully, rather than blame themselves or others; to build tolerance for frustration, rather than be a victim of the demands of self and others —in short, to help the child become more rationally self-controlled and disciplined by being equitable disciplinarians themselves.

DISCIPLINE AS VIEWED BY RET

It is the goal of RET to foster self-interest, self-direction, tolerance, acceptance of uncertainty, and flexibility in children while attempting to minimize hostility and anxiety. Within an RET framework, the function of discipline is to help children achieve these goals by acquiring inner controls and self-discipline in order to facilitate the transition from outer-directed to inner-directed and self-responsible human beings, who are free to choose how to best lead their own lives. Discipline is therefore defined as the use of control to achieve a desired end. In RET, the best control is seen as self-control; however, because children have not, by and large, acquired the capacity for self-control, they are dependent on the adults in their lives initially to apply external controls, which they will ultimately internalize. Since the desired goal of discipline within an RET framework is self-enhancement and happiness, between control and the goal had best come rational thinking, for one important attribute of rational thinking is that it helps to achieve desired ends. RET therefore views discipline as an ongoing process involving cognitive- and behavioral-skill acquisition and emotional growth, rather than as a series of single interventions whose only goal is the termination of obnoxious behavior. The concept of discipline *as a skill* to be taught, rather than as a restriction to be placed, is ultimately a more health-inducing practice because it enables both adult and child to view the process as one designed to lead to ongoing growth, rather than to ongoing restriction or condemnation. If the adult clearly communicates to the child that discipline is being administered to help him learn how to be relatively happy and achieve his goals, the message from adult to child becomes "You have done something wrong and I would like to help you learn how to do better in the future," rather than "You are naughty and must be punished."

Arnold Lazarus mentions that his most severely disturbed adult patients report a history of "over discipline in the absence of love, coupled with harsh criticism, rejection, and inconsistent parental behavior" (Lazarus, 1971, p. 202), as well as unstructured permissiveness. Additionally, Coopersmith has concluded: "The most general statement about the antecedents of self-esteem can be given in terms of three conditions: (1) total or nearly total acceptance of the children by their parents; (2) clearly defined and enforced limits; and (3) the respect and latitude for individual action that exists within the defined limits" (Coopersmith, 1967, p. 236). RET advocates agree with these points of view for determining appropriate approaches to disciplining children and youth.

RET APPROACHES TO CHILDREN

Parents' and Teachers' Irrational Ideas

Before I discuss disciplinary methods and issues, it is

important to stress that disciplining adults must take a sharp, close look at themselves to determine if their behaviors and words are communicating a rational message to their children. Not only does thinking clearly, feeling appropriately, and behaving productively serve as a good model for children, who are likely to give back to adults the treatment they themselves have received, it also makes discipline and all other adult-child interactions most effective.

For a start, parents might examine each of the previously presented irrational beliefs, select those that might be applicable to them, and determine how each might function to sabotage their efforts to be good disciplinarians. If one is not thinking rationally, behaviors will likely be self-defeating. Here are a few examples of how irrational beliefs may contribute to poor child management. 1. *The idea that it is a dire necessity for an adult to be loved or approved by virtually every significant person in his community.* The parent or teacher who holds this irrational belief has adopted a no-win strategy for himself, as he would find it very difficult to apply appropriate disciplinary measures consistently for fear of losing the child's love and admiration. The adult who needs to please the child, and so is overly indulgent in an attempt to win his love, will only attain a position of impotence in the management of the child. Children quickly learn to manipulate such an adult, to make their love contingent upon getting what they want from the adult; as a result the child ends up ruling the roost or the classroom. Meanwhile the parent or teacher has not taught the child self-discipline or frustration tolerance.

This adult probably also has a need for approval from other adults, as well as from his children; perhaps he thinks that others rate him on how well his children behave. This adult is really in a double-bind if, for instance, the child misbehaves at a friend's home. If he disciplines the child, the child will become hateful, but if the adult does not discipline the child, the friend will likely conclude that he is a rotten parent. Neither outcome can be tolerated.

A necessary part of parenting and disciplining involves setting limits, employing penalties, and encouraging children to do what is good, but perhaps distasteful, for them. As a consequence of teaching and disciplining children, it is inevitable that adults will sometimes be viewed by their children with scorn and displeasure. The adult who overreacts to these responses and exaggerates their importance will be less effective than one who can stand firm, not to be manipulated by the child into a position of self-downing, and keep the long-range goal of discipline in mind. After all, aren't there also times when adults don't like children either?

2. *The idea that one should be thoroughly competent and achieving in all possible respects to consider oneself worthwhile.* To be the perfect parent is the impossible dream, unless of course one is blessed with the perfect child. The catch-22 for the perfect parent is, of course, that there are no perfect children, and no matter how hard this parent tries to be the perfect disciplinarian, the perfect role model, or the perfect friend to his children, they will without fail make mistakes, have problems, or even reject the parent. Because the perfect parent interprets any imperfection in his children as proof of his own worthlessness, the result is usually a parent full of guilt, self-blame, and self-downing over not being a good and worthwhile parent.

In addition, the adult who thinks he has to be perfect will probably (1) not take risks for fear of failure and (2) down himself when a mistake is made. He will therefore be a poor model for the child in the self-disciplined pursuit of difficult goals. The message here is: "If you can't do it perfectly, don't do it at all; it's awful and horrible to make a mistake." If this belief is also held about the child, the adult may penalize or even punish any unsuccessful or incompetent behavior on the part of the child, thus conveying the message: "If you do things badly, you are a bad person."

A child who steadfastly adopts his parents' model of perfection will probably severely restrict his life. If it is believed that doing things badly equals "bad me," the child will not learn to tolerate the discomfort of mistake-making and will strive never to be a mistake-maker or to let anyone know if a mistake is made. Failure is to be avoided at all costs.

Because all human beings are by nature imperfect mistake-makers, it is guaranteed that somewhere along the line both adults and children are going to "mess up." When this happens it is far better to accept the mishap, learn what one can from it to avoid its happening again in the future, and go on from there. When adults can calmly and rationally accept their own shortcomings while continuing to build their strengths, they are providing children with a realistic model for growth.

3. *The idea that human happiness is externally caused and that people have little or no ability to control their sorrows or disturbances.* The adult who complains that the children are driving him crazy, or that they make him mad, is abdicating his responsibility for controlling his own feelings. In essence he is saying: "I have no power to control how I feel, but my children do have the power to manipulate my feelings." This sounds like a parent who has given up trying to teach long-term goals and has opted for a position of passivity. This adult probably blames not only his children, but all other people and the universe as well, for his own uncomfortable feelings and unfortunate circumstances.

It is preferable for adults to recognize that they alone are responsible for how they feel and can choose to feel in self-enhancing, as opposed to self-defeating, ways. This realization will enable them to become more effective disciplinarians and to provide their children with a model of responsibility.

4. *The idea that if something is or could be dangerous or fearsome, one should be terribly concerned about it and should keep dwelling on the possibility of its occurring.* While it is true that child rearing is a much more risky business these days than it used to be, it is self-defeating for adults to spend a good part of their time worrying about all the dangers which might engulf their children. An ounce of worry, for that matter a pound of worry, doesn't produce a gram of prevention. What it does produce is worried, fearful children who are reluctant to take the risks involved in growth and who view life as an accident waiting to happen, rather than as an opportunity for enjoyment. On the other hand, this sort of child rearing could also produce a child who is so disgusted with his parents' admonitions that he or she rebels, becomes reckless, and takes irresponsible and dangerous risks, thus giving the parents a dose of what they most feared.

There are dangers inherent in living, but if one constantly catastrophizes over them, they grow out of all proportion until they consume. If, on the other hand, one realistically recognizes the dangers, is concerned but not worried, takes proper precautions against the undesirable thing's happening, and then focuses attention elsewhere, life can be productively lived, rather than destructively avoided. One can be a concerned parent without being a worried and fearful parent.

5. *The world must treat me fairly and others should do what I want them to do.* This belief places the adult in a

position equivalent to the child's predisciplined state of egocentricism. An adult who continues to hold this belief would childishly demand that children always be obedient, do what the adult wants them to, and never behave in unexpected or undisciplined ways. This demonstrates a basic ignorance on the part of the adult as to the nature of child behavior and an unrealistic demand that children behave in certain ways. It also indicates a lack of awareness of the long-range goal of discipline, which is to build self-control in the child. Consequently this parent is likely to punish a child on the basis of his or her own short-term comfort rather than on that of long-term gain, without helping the child learn to behave in more self-disciplined ways.

The nature of the child is egocentric, and so children naturally believe that they should get what they want, when they want it. A child who continues to cling to this irrational belief and is not helped to give it up is setting him- or herself up for many frustrations and disappointments, for the world does not function according to our wishes and demands and others don't always do what we want. It would be kindest to teach all children to tolerate the discomfort which comes from not getting what they want and to give up the demand that things must go their way.

These examples demonstrate how irrational thinking can make it difficult for adults to employ effective disciplinary measures. It would be good for adults to help themselves and their children give up irrational beliefs that interfere with optimal functioning; while realizing that the individual himself, for good or ill, intervenes between environmental input and emotional output, and so has enormous potential to control feelings and behaviors. The first step in giving up irrational ideas is to determine which beliefs are functioning to determine behavior in maladaptive ways. The second step is to actively challenge and dispute these ideas by questioning their validity. One might pose such questions as: Where is the evidence that if I make a mistake I am totally worthless and incapable of ever doing the right thing? Why is it awful if others don't like me? Why should I always get my way? A third step might include an attempt to stick to empirical reality by campaigning against the use of all catastrophic words (such as *awful, terrible, horrible*, etc.) and all absolute and demand words (such as *should, ought, must*, etc.) that get one into trouble by feeding and sustaining irrational beliefs. In short, the RET position maintains that realism is at the core of a good philosophy of discipline, that awareness of real and logical situations and outcomes, as opposed to unrealistic and irrational demands and beliefs, is essential to the creation and implementation of such a philosophy of discipline.

Characteristics of RET Discipline

1. Why discipline? RET views human beings as having an innate tendency to think irrationally, to avoid frustration and discomfort, and to easily upset themselves. If left to their own devices and allowed to remain in an essentially undisciplined and permissive state, most children grow up into lazy, whining, self-defeating adults, incapable of getting the good things in life. Most children are incapable and undesirous of disciplining themselves, or learning self-control. It is important that they be helped to learn these skills for their own benefit and for the attainment of future goals. Therefore, a good reason to discipline a child or youth would be to aid him in the acquisition of self-management and critical-thinking skills.

An additional reason to discipline children is to help them learn to give up short-term pleasure for long-term gain. This is a difficult lesson for children and youth to learn, for they tend to focus on the joys of immediate gratification and short-term gain. Only as they grow older and experience the increasing gratification that can come from tolerating the discomfort of waiting for the payoff, can they achieve self-discipline. In essence, this is a matter of converting one's belief about an uncomfortable situation from "I can't stand it, it's awful" to "It's uncomfortable, but not unbearable, and will eventually get me something worth waiting for." To help children and youth get a more concrete understanding of the ramifications of self-discipline, the adult might point out that discipline usually requires some degree of self-deprivation. Further, if significant adults model self-discipline, the child is more likely to acquire self-controlled behavioral patterns.

2. *Discipline by whom?* Because human beings are born into this world essentially undisciplined and without self-control, it is the role of adults, who have, it is hoped, already acquired self-control and discipline, to teach these skills to the growing child. Young children initially require many interventions by adults who can help them learn to discriminate between appropriate and safe behaviors and inappropriate or dangerous behaviors and who can also help them learn to predict the outcome or consequences of their behaviors. Thus an overly permissive parent who gives a child freedom to make all his own decisions is not helping that child to learn how to discipline and control himself.

3. *Individual factors.* It is important for the adult to consider the constantly developing capabilities of the child and consequently to adjust the frequency and quality of the disciplinary intervention to the child's growing capacity for self-management. As children develop, they exhibit increasingly less egocentricism. Childish thought is

characterized by egocentricism, absolutism, grandiosity, and magical ideas (Ellis et al., 1975), all of which seem to decrease as the child matures cognitively. Whereas a five-year-old cannot understand a parent's argument against going to the circus, the child between the ages of eight and eleven is more able to comprehend another person's viewpoint. With age and experience, through a process of cognitive restructuring, social interaction, and constant confrontation with opposing views, the child gradually develops a sense of perspective and the ability to assimilate and accommodate other viewpoints. The adult's understanding of the cognitive-development sequence of the child might provide more realistic expectations of the child's abilities at certain developmental stages and, therefore, also provide better understanding of what might be the most effective and efficient means of teaching the child the principles of self-discipline.

Since it is unrealistic to expect children to acquire self-discipline skills early and easily, it is important to help them by adjusting the interventions and rules to suit the needs of the particular child. It is realistic to assume that a younger child will require more adult supervision and intervention and that an older child will require increasingly less direct adult supervision as he or she becomes increasingly adept at self-supervision.

It is also important to remember that there are vast differences in *temperament* among children that are evident at birth (Thomas et al., 1965). To be maximally effective, the adult had better try to assess the child's unique temperament by observing his patterns of reaction and then disciplining him accordingly. Even a mild reminder to a shy child, that he hasn't introduced a friend to his parents, may bring that child to feel guilty and shameful and to react with even greater shyness in the future; a less vulnerable child will be impervious to such criticism.

4. *Penalty versus punishment.* Ellis makes a vital distinction between *penalty* and *punishment*. He reasons that punishment is intended to devalue a person's sense of self-worth. Punishment is usually a hateful attack on the person. On the other hand a penalty is a limit or frustration which communicates to the child that his or her behavior has surpassed the bounds of what is acceptable. Punishment is destructive. A penalty is often a necessary and logical consequence in real life (Ellis, 1975). While it is important for adults to be firm and consistent in disciplining their children, the disciplinary measures employed had best be a logical consequence of the misbehavior, rather than a punishment unrelated to the unacceptable act. For example, to deny a child a privilege such as going away to camp for the summer because he does not keep his room neat enough, becomes not a logical penalty for sloppiness but a form of parental retaliation which will not teach the child to be neater in the future, but will be likely to stir up resentment and feelings of injustice. Instead, the parents might not allow the child to have friends over to visit unless his room is in order, thus rewarding him by permitting friends to visit when his room is in a presentable condition. In short, discipline is *not the same as punishment;* the purpose of discipline is to teach self-control, and it can include a system of rewards for appropriate behavior, as well as a system of penalties for inappropriate behavior. Punishment, on the other hand, is the negative application of power designed to stop obnoxious behavior.

As a consequence of this point of view, spanking and other forms of corporal punishment are generally discouraged. In spanking a child most parents cannot help but direct an enormous amount of anger at a child, which can be very harmful. Even in the unusual cases where spanking is effective in controlling behavior, emotions that are associated with the behavior may be submerged. Hatred may dwell hidden awaiting a potentially explosive release. Finally, spanking interferes with the opportunity to confront the irrational beliefs that may underlie the misbehavior. Spanking is coercion in which the opportunity to convey both an educational message regarding the reason for the misbehavior and constructive alternatives is often lost (Ellis, 1975).

There may be times when a spank or light slap may be called for, especially in young children who would find verbal intervention less effective—for example, to teach a two-year-old not to touch a hot stove or run out into the street. If used at all, however, corporal punishment had best be used only as a last resort, and only if it can be administered *without anger*. As stated previously, RET advocates view anger as the emotional consequence of making an irrational, childish demand on oneself, on others, or on the universe: that they *not* be the way they are or do what already has been done. Not only is this sort of demand self-defeating, for it leads to emotional upset and loss of control, it provides a poor model for the child as well. An adult who punishes out of anger is in essence saying to the child: "I, an adult, am out of control and demand that you, a child, be in control." Such inconsistent messages are difficult for a child to understand and benefit from.

In disciplining a child, one should not give the child the feeling that he is being reprimanded because the adult thinks he is a "bad" human being who deserves to suffer. A better message is that although he has misbehaved, he is still an acceptable human being capable of doing better in the future. In other words, it is best to bring a child's misbehavior to his attention, while applying penalties and rewards if necessary. It is best, however, to do this in a way by which the child can understand that he or she is acceptable as a person, but that the particular behavior in question is not. It is therefore important for adults to provide children with good models of self-accepting, nonblaming behaviors.

Framework for Undertaking Rational-Emotive Discipline

Discipline can best be implemented as part of an ongoing strategy geared to promote the acquisition of self-control and self-management skills. It is advisable in the immediate situation that the adult keep in mind the long-range goal of discipline, teaching the child to be self-disciplined. This is often difficult to accomplish when the short-range goal is to stop the child's currently obnoxious behavior. However, discipline that is primarily geared to the adult's mood or short-range comfort, rather than to the child's age, temperament, or ability or to the harmfulness of the misbehavior, becomes erratic and difficult for the child to understand or profit from.

Consequently it is best to have a *predetermined criteria* for judging the acceptability of a behavior and a policy for dealing with violations. Behaviors which are self-destructive (playing in the street for a toddler, playing with matches, etc.), injurious to others (kicking, biting, pushing, etc.), or damaging to the personal property of others are clearly not acceptable. Other behaviors, however, may be more subtle, less blatantly inappropriate, and more difficult to assess. A basic criteria in determining the acceptability of a behavior might be whether it is helpful to the child in learning self-control, learning to think critically and rationally, and growing into a healthy adult.

For the child to benefit most from disciplinary rules and limits, it is best to make them clear, concise, concrete, and consistently applied. It is important that an adult have clear rules and limits in mind and to communicate them as simply and concretely as possible to the child, so that both acceptable and unacceptable behaviors are understood by both parent and child. It is also wise to explain to the child why certain behavior is unacceptable and other behavior is more desirable: "You are not permitted to play with matches because it could be dangerous for you and for others" is easier for a child to understand and accept than the command, "Don't play with matches," which is somewhat intimidating and could possibly be intriguing to an adventurous child. It is important to make the consequences of violating rules and limits both clearly known and consistently applied. A child will be more likely to follow a rule, say, about going to bed at eight o'clock each night, if he (1) knows what the rule is, (2) knows why the rule has been made, (3) knows what the consequences of rule violation would be (for example, going to bed earlier the next night), and (4) knows that there is no chance that he can get away with rule violation. If this procedure is followed, the child is not only being disciplined, but learning to discipline himself. As the result of a preplanned formula for the administration of discipline, the child can more easily learn to discriminate between appropriate and inappropriate behavior and to predict the consequences of engaging in inappropriate behavior. Ultimately the child has the *choice* of whether or not to be disciplined, but must always pay the consequences for violating the limits.

GUIDELINES FOR UNDERSTANDING
RATIONAL-EMOTIVE DISCIPLINE

Many parents are able to plan a strategy of discipline, set limits, arrange for logical consequences and other penalties, and calmly explain the disciplinary procedures to their children. However, in the heat of the moment, the best made disciplinary plans of parents and teachers seem to evaporate, and they often find themselves resorting to the same strategies and techniques they have always used, accompanied by the same old feelings of incompetence, self-downing, and frustration they have always felt. To help the adult avoid the pitfall of resorting to automatic and habitual forms of discipline that have been ineffective in the past and that continue to be ineffective in the present, the following strategy is offered. This will help adults to make the transition from irrational to rationally thinking and reacting disciplinarians. It is designed to help adults clear up any remaining irrationalities in their own thinking that might interfere with the application of a preplanned strategy for disciplining their children, while also helping them to follow through on their plans.

When faced with a situation calling for disciplinary intervention, the first thing is to remember to pause before doing anything and check out the situation using the following guidelines. These guidelines are offered for use as well in the conceptualization and evaluation of a good strategy of discipline. They are presented as an aid to adults who wish to analyze how they are functioning as disciplinarians, so they may decide if their goals are valid and if they are achieving their goals and to determine ways in which they may be more effective as disciplinarians. They also enable the adult to view the situation from the perspective of the child. The guidelines are presented as a series of questions that can be asked and answered by the adult about his own and his child's behaviors.

From the point of view of the child
1. What behaviors are being exhibited?
2. What is the child's goal? What is the child trying to accomplish by this behavior?
3. What might the child be thinking?

4. What might the child be feeling?
5. How does the child want me to respond?

From the point of view of the adult
1. What is my goal in this situation? What am I trying to accomplish (long-term and short-term goals)?
2. What are my thoughts and beliefs about this behavior?
3. What are my feelings?
4. What are my behaviors? How am I attempting to achieve my goal (a) by disputing irrational beliefs and (b) by my actions?
5. How can I help this child build self-discipline in this area?

The following two examples are offered to demonstrate how these guidelines might be used in practice.

Suppose your seven-year-old son has been chronically lying for the past few months. You persistently point out to him the undesirability of his behavior and try to help him learn to distinguish between truth and falsehood, but his lying still continues. One evening his teacher phones you and asks if you have received the notes she has sent you by way of your son, requesting a meeting with you. You haven't received any notes. After hanging up the phone, you call in your child and ask him if he has any notes to you from his teacher, and he says no. At this point, as such emotions as anger, despair, and resentment possibly begin to well, it would be a good idea to pause and consider the situation within the previously presented guidelines, before acting or disciplining the child.

From the point of view of the child
1. What behaviors are being exhibited?

He is not telling the truth. He is not giving me the notes from the teacher, and he is denying their existence.
2. What is the child's goal?
It seems that the child is probably trying to avoid punishment. He is frightened of the consequences of what he has done and perhaps is also frightened of making a mistake. Could this be the motivation for his lying in other situations as well?
3. What might the child be thinking?
"It would be awful if my parents and teacher found out that I destroyed those notes, and it would be awful if my teacher told my parents how badly I'm doing in school. I couldn't stand it if I were punished."
4. What might the child be feeling?
Anxious, guilty, ashamed, frightened.
5. How does the child want me to respond?
Ideally the child would want me to be sympathetic and understanding.

From the point of view of the parent
1. What is my goal in this situation?
I would like my child to learn to tell the truth and take the consequences.
2. What are my thoughts and beliefs about this behavior?
"My child shouldn't ever lie. It's awful if he deceives me. After all I've done to help him get over this problem, it shouldn't continue. His teacher must think I'm a rotten parent and that's awful. Maybe I really am a rotten parent and that's even worse."
3. What are my feelings?
Anger, resentment, despair, self-downing.
4. What are my behaviors?
(a) Disputing irrational beliefs: "Although I don't like it, there is really no reason why he shouldn't lie. It

really isn't awful that he lies, merely unfortunate. It's too bad that my efforts to help him haven't worked, but not terrible. Even if the teacher does think I'm a rotten parent, it doesn't mean that I have to get upset, or that I really am rotten as a parent. And even if I am a rotten parent, I don't have to put myself down and feel miserable, that's not helping me improve or helping my child to stop lying."

(b) Actions: Tell the child that I have spoken to his teacher and know that he hasn't been delivering the notes given him. Tell him that I do not approve of this *behavior*, but that I still love and accept *him*. Let him know that I understand how difficult it is at times to tell the truth, but that it is important. I shall also tell him that I expect him to go to school tomorrow and inform his teacher that he has not been taking home the notes and ask for another. This is a logical penalty for having lied and been deceptive. Also I shall try and provide my son with a better model of a truth-telling individual.

5. How can I help this child build self-discipline?

This child appears to require help in accepting the consequences of his actions and help in accepting himself as imperfect. Positive attention given to all truthful statements and to all attempts at doing difficult tasks (rather than negative attention to lies and positive attention or negative attention for outcomes or results) will probably help reduce the lying behavior, increase self-confidence, and help remove some of the risk involved in facing the consequences of his behavior, which the lie was designed to help him avoid.

Your eleven-year-old son and eight-year-old daughter are constantly fighting whenever they are together. You usually yell and scream back at them trying to get them to stop fighting. This is usually successful for a little while, but after a few minutes of peace, the fighting resumes with even greater ferocity. One evening you return home after a long day at work and are greeted by the angry snarls of your fighting children. Rather than immediately jumping into the fracas, you pause and consider the following:

From the point of view of the child
1. What behaviors are being exhibited?
The children are yelling, shouting, calling each other names, and kicking and pinching each other.
2. What are their goals?
Each child wants to get his or her own way, and both probably want my attention. Perhaps they are bored and fighting is more interesting than doing homework.
3. What are they thinking?
"I should have what I want when I want it. I want mother and father to notice me."
4. What are they feeling?
Angry, hostile.
5. How do they want me to respond?
The children want me to intercede — that is one of their goals.

From the point of view of the adult
1. What is my goal in this situation?
A short-term goal is to get them to stop fighting. Long-term goals are to help them learn (a) self-discipline, (b) how to handle disputes calmly, and (c) how to respect and cooperate with one another.
2. What are my thoughts?
"They shouldn't be fighting. I can't stand it when they carry on like this. It is awful that they don't love and respect each other. Where have I gone wrong?"

3. What am I feeling?

Angry, despairing, self-downing.

4. What are my behaviors?

(a) Disputing irrational beliefs: Why shouldn't they fight? I don't like it but that doesn't mean that it shouldn't be. After all, I yell and scream a lot too, and I do pay attention to them when they fight. Since getting my attention is one of their goals, it is logical that they continue to fight. I wish they got along better, but it is not the end of the world that they don't. Even if I have handled this badly in the past, self-downing won't improve conditions or make them stop fighting.

(b) Actions: Since one goal of the fighting is to get my attention, I will calmly announce to both children that henceforth I will not pay attention to either of them when they are fighting. I will do this without anger and pay a lot of attention to them when they are calm and unbellicose. I will try to teach them how to settle their disputes without getting angry and how to control their feelings by thinking more rationally. I will treat them with respect and will not yell or scream at them anymore, and they will likely learn to respect each other, and maybe even me.

5. How can I help them build self-discipline in this area?

I can best help them by ignoring undisciplined and aggressive behavior, giving positive attention for disciplined and peaceful behavior, and try to be a good role model myself.

In conclusion, RET views discipline at its best as a humanistically applied technique of communication, teaching, and interaction, designed to enhance the development of self-control and critical-thinking skills. Consequently, the role of the adult as disciplinarian is to help the child "become an independently thinking, instead of a dependently suggestible, self-controller" (Ellis et al., 1975, p. 136). When administered in accordance with the rules of logic and rational thinking, and the desire to help oneself or another, discipline can be an effective means of enabling an individual ultimately to lead a happier, more productive life.

REFERENCES

Coopersmith, S. (1967), *Antecedents of Self-Esteem.* San Francisco: Freeman.

Daly, S. (1971), Using reason with deprived pre-school children. *Rational Living,* 5(2):12–19.

Ellis, A. (1957), Rational psychotherapy and individual psychology. *J. of Individual Psychol.,* 13:38–44.

_____ (1962a), Rational-Emotive Psychotherapy. Paper presented at the symposium: Approaches in Counseling and Psychotherapy: Similarities and Differences. American Psychological Association Convention, St. Louis, Missouri.

_____ (1962b), *Reason and Emotion in Psychotherapy.* New York: Lyle Stuart.

_____ (1969), Teaching emotional education in the classroom. *School Health Review,* November 10–14.

_____ (1971), Rational-Emotive Psychotherapy and Its Application to Emotional Education. Paper delivered at the 17th International Congress of the International Association of Applied Psychology, Liege, Belgium, July.

_____ (1973a), Emotional education at the living school. In: *Counseling Children in Groups,* ed. M. M. Ohlsen. New York: Holt, Rinehart & Winston, pp. 79–94.

_____ (1973b), *Humanistic Psychotherapy: The Rational-Emotive Approach.* New York: Julian Press.

_____ (1973c), My philosophy of psychotherapy. *J. of Contempor. Psychoth.,* 6(1):13–18.

_____ (1974), Experience and rationality: The making of a rational-emotive therapist. *Psychotherapy,* 11(3):194–198.

_____ (1975), *How to Live with a Neurotic at Home and Work.* New York: Crown.

_____ Moseley, S., and Wolfe, J. L. (1975), *How to Raise an Emotionally Healthy, Happy Child.* Hollywood: Wilshire.

Hauck, P. A. (1973), *The Rational Management of Children.* New York: Libra.

Knaus, W. (1974), *Rational-Emotive Education: A Manual for Elementary School Teachers.* New York: Institute for Rational Living.

Lazarus, A. A. (1971), *Behavior Therapy and Beyond.* New York: McGraw-Hill.

Thomas, R., Chess, S., and Birch, H. G. (1965), *Your Child Is a Person.* New York: Viking.

Young, H. S. (1974), *A Rational Counseling Primer.* New York: Institute for Rational Living.

RECOMMENDED READINGS

Brody, M. (1973), Rational-emotive affective education techniques. Mimeographed paper, Temple University.

Brody, M. (1974), The Effect of the Rational-Emotive Affective Education Approach on Anxiety, Frustration Tolerance, and Self-Esteem with Fifth-Grade Students. Unpublished doctoral dissertation, Temple University.

Ellis, A., and Harper, R. A. (1972), *A Guide to Rational Living.* Hollywood: Wilshire.

Glicken, M. D. (1969), Rational counseling: A new approach to children. *J. of Elem. Guid. and Coun.,* 2(4):261–267.

Lafferty, C., Denneral, D., and Rettich, P. (1964), A creative school mental health program. *Nat. Elem. Sch. Principal,* 43:28–35.

Meichenbaum, D. H. (1971), *Cognitive Factors in Behavior Modification: Modifying What Clients Say to Themselves.* Waterloo, Canada: University of Waterloo Press.

Whiteman, M. (1967), Children's conception of psychological causality. *Child Development,* 38:143–155.

5

Discipline:
A Transactional-Analytic View

James G. Allen, M.D.
Barbara A. Allen, A.C.S.W., Ph.D.

Transactional Analysis encompasses a theory of personality structure, a theory of intrapsychic and interpersonal functioning, and a system of psychotherapy. It was elaborated in the years following 1956 by Eric Berne, a psychiatrist, in that area between Big Sur and San Francisco which has been so rich in psychotherapeutic innovation and in humanistic psychology.

TA, as it is colloquially called, developed as a variant of social psychiatry (Berne, 1964; Jongeward, 1973). Berne himself saw it as an extension of psychoanalysis — a view not shared by many psychoanalysts. It now encompasses a large body of theory and a number of divergent treatment techniques incorporating much of what was useful in older approaches (Allen, J. R., and Allen, 1972, 1978; Berne, 1964, 1972). However, it is still flexible and still growing. Recently, it has been adapted for work with psychotic patients and hard-core sociopaths in the maximum security units of penitentiaries (Berne,

1972). Research studies have been limited but encouraging — some of the most notable being conducted by the California Youth Authority and by Lieberman and Yalom at Stanford (Allen, J. G., 1973; Allen, J. G., and Webb, 1975; Lieberman et al., 1973; McCormick, 1973; Price, 1975; Thomas et al., 1968). Most recently, transactional analysts have begun to look not at hypothetical reconstructions of the childhood experiences of adult patients, but at real children themselves as they grow and decide the directions of their lives. In this chapter the basic concepts of TA will be summarized as briefly as possible, after which the contributions of TA to discipline will be discussed.

Traditionally, TA theory has been subdivided into four parts.

     I. Analysis of the personality structure — Structural Analysis

    II. Analysis of a transaction between people, or between various parts of the self — Transactional Analysis proper

   III. Analysis of a specific type of transaction — Game Analysis

   IV. Analysis of a person's life-plan — Script Analysis

I. Structural Analysis

The human personality can be conceptualized as consisting of three separate subselves or ego-states. Each of these ego-states is a particular set of ways of thinking, feeling, and behaving that go together. These three patterns of defining reality, processing information, and reacting to the world are designated *Parent, Adult,* and *Child.*

At times we respond to events in the present as if they were identical to ones in the past. We think, act, and feel as we did at an earlier age. These particular ego-states, or "inner children of the past," may be loving, spontaneous, frightened, or angry. When we energize any of these, we are said to be in a Child ego-state.

At times we look objectively at the facts, estimate probable consequences of certain actions, and consider cause and effect and the most appropriate behavior in a rational, calm, and unemotional manner. When we do this, we are said to be in our Adult ego-state.

At times we respond like our parents or other significant adults in our childhood. When we think, act, and feel like these people who raised us — as we experienced them — we are said to be in a Parent ego-state.

It is important to understand that each of these ego-states is real and observable. They are not hypothetical constructs like the id, ego, and superego of psychoanalysis. A person is in his Child when he acts, thinks, and feels as he really did at a younger age. His experience may be "Wow! This is just the way I felt when I was little." Perhaps his parents may even be able to tell him at what age he acted this way.

These three ego-states allow us much flexibility in dealing with the world around us, and they account for many apparent inconsistencies in our behavior. No ego-state is better than any other. The mature person manifests each of these and uses them all, depending on their appropriateness for the situation; he is not stuck in his Adult. We diagram the normal human personality as shown at the top of page 102.

Certain people — often doctors, ministers, and other "people helpers" — are usually in their Parent. Other people — "clowns," "crybabies," and "clinging vines" — are usually in their Child.

II. Transactional Analysis

Between the time we are born and the time we die,

Structural Analysis: The Normal Person

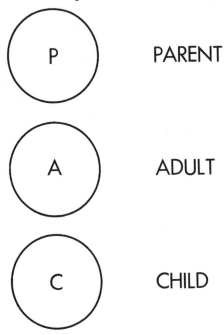

PARENT

ADULT

CHILD

we must do something, together with others or alone. There are six main ways of structuring time. In order of increasing richness, excitement, and risk, these are:

1. Withdrawal	4. Activities
2. Rituals	5. Games
3. Pastimes	6. Intimacy

Transactions usually proceed in series. The simplest forms are procedures (a series of transactions aimed at getting something done) and rituals (a stereotyped series of complementary transactions programmed by social forces). Our morning greeting, "Hi," is an example of a ritual—pleasant in itself, but disconcerting if our proposed partner does not reciprocate. Pastimes are, as the name suggests, simply ways of spending time, with small talk, often of a fill-in-the-blank type—such as, "I like _____ better than _____," or "Ever been to _____?" Games, on the other hand, consist of a series of complementary hidden transactions leading to some well-defined and predictable outcome. Because of the responses the games produce and the associated excitement, children in some families learn to spend a lot of time playing games.

Using the framework of structural analysis, it is possible to diagram what happens between two individuals. For example, a student may ask his teacher what chapter he is responsible for in the history textbook. This may be asked in a very straight, factual way and the teacher may reply in a straight, factual way, giving the required information. This series of transactions can be diagrammed as shown at the top of page 104.

Because the student's question is factual and without emotion and since he apparently is seeking pure information, we would say he is transacting from his Adult. Because the teacher responds without emotion and in a purely fact-giving manner, we draw her response from her Adult to his Adult.

A second student, however, is a very different kind of young man. From childhood, he has expected the "big" people to look after him and has never learned to take responsibility for himself or even to remember what he needs to know. He may ask the question from his Child. In this case, he would be coming on as he did when he really was a child, trying to get the teacher to take care of him the way his mother and father used to. He is coming on from his Child and trying to contact the teacher's Parent. If the teacher responds by parenting him and giving him the information in a nurturant, warm way or in an angry, critical way, much as she would to a young child, she responds from her Parent to his Child. This series of transactions would be diagrammed as shown on the top of page 105.

Adult-Adult Transaction

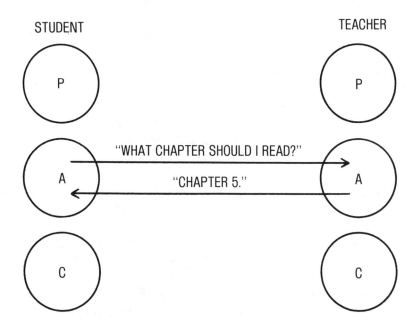

Sometimes people do things outside of their aware-ness. For example, the young man in the above instance may have consciously been aware only of asking for Adult information. However, at another level and out of his awareness, he may have come across like a young child trying to get parental attention. In this instance, we have two sets of messages, the overt one and the covert one. Using dashes to indicate the covert message, we would diagram this transaction, which is also an example of the transference phenomenon of which Dr. Cass writes, as shown on page 106.

III. Game Analysis

Games are a very special type of transaction. They

Child-Parent Transaction

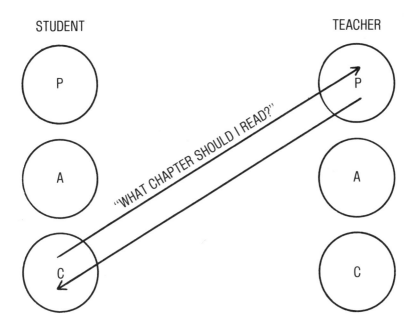

STUDENT   TEACHER

"WHAT CHAPTER SHOULD I READ?"

are a predictable series of transactions with a hidden agenda. People play games to keep the world and the people in it predictable. Games help reinforce the decisions we made when we were a child. They reinforce the basic positions and attitudes we have taken about ourselves and others. They help us collect or hand out the kind of feelings we have grown used to.

Games can be analyzed in a number of ways. They involve discounts and a shift in roles. However, for practical purposes they may be defined as a series of transactions where:

1. There is an ostensible message.
2. There is a hidden (secret or unconscious) message.
3. There is a response by the game partner to the secret message.

Overt and Covert Transactions

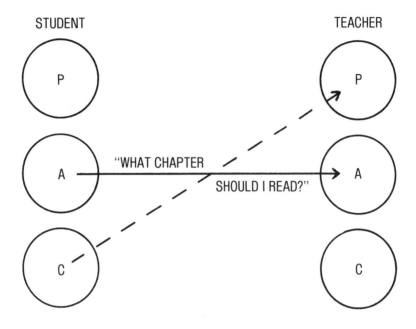

4. The person who sets up the game switches roles.
5. The person who sets up the game has the sudden-surprise "bad" feeling.

All games follow this predictable sequence.

Games are generally named after the feeling the person who initiates them has when the game is finished. Thus, when the person feels bad and "kicked," the game is called "Kick Me."

Example: Johnny, age three, was alone in the living room while his parents were enjoying coffee with neighbors in the kitchen. Suddenly, there was a crash. His mother went into the living room to find Johnny standing beside the remnants of her favorite vase, tears in his eyes.

Mother: "Who did that?"

Johnny: "Suzy [the dog]."

Mother knew she had let Suzy out the door five minutes before. For a moment she stood there. Slowly, the back of her neck began to flush. She stepped forward and hit Johnny, saying: "If there is one thing I can't stand, it's a liar!" This mother is not an ogre, but an average, caring woman. However, she did set Johnny up to lie, even if she was not aware of it. The question, "Who did that?" was an invitation to lie — and Johnny complied. This particular game is called NIGYSOB — "Now I've Got You, You Son-of-a-Bitch," because that is how the mother feels when it is over. We can analyze the above incident as follows:

1. Overt transaction (mother): "Who did that?" Ostensibly, the mother is just asking for facts; that is, this is a question coming from her Adult and aimed at Johnny's Adult.

2. Hidden Transaction (mother): Given the circumstances, it is very likely that Johnny broke the vase. To ask "Who did that?" is to invite him to lie.

3. Response to the hidden transaction (Johnny): "Suzy." At this point Johnny might have said he did it and there would have been no game. Johnny had to be willing to participate.

4. Switch (mother): As the mother stood there immobile, the back of her neck began to get red. She switched from being aware of asking a question and finding out the facts (Adult), to righteous indignation (Parent).

5. A surprise "bad" feeling (mother): The mother did not intend to catch Johnny. Consequently, her anger was a surprise to her. Had she consciously set out to catch him she would not have been surprised; this would not have been a game, but rather, an activity.

Mother ends up righteously angry and can use this feeling to justify earlier decisions about herself, others, and her fate. In the process, however, she has been teaching Johnny how to get attention, how to act when angry or surprised (hit), how to solve problems (hit), and what is expected of him (to lie). Johnny would not have been a "discipline problem" at all, if he had not been set up.

In addition to NIGYSOB, some other games common to child rearing are summarized.

1. Kick Me
2. Cops and Robbers
3. If Only It Weren't for You
4. Uproar
5. Poor Me
6. I'm Only Trying to Help

Kick Me. The person who sets up this game is secretly asking to be hurt (kicked) and is then surprised when it happens. For example, if the teenager who turns the corner on two wheels in front of a police car feels hurt when apprehended, he has successfully played "Kick Me." He can now use these hurt feelings to feel that he is no good and that the police are bad. This game may be played as "Kill Me." Most people who are murdered are done in not by strangers, but by friends and relatives.

If the player plays this game at an intellectual level, doing dumb things that irk others enough to call him "Stupid," the game is called "Stupid."

Cops and Robbers. This game combines both NIGYSOB and "Kick Me" and is played by a number of players: the juvenile delinquent who is "it," the police, parents, lawyers, and judges. The payoff is for "it" to get caught. In the meantime, there is great excitement for all and many opportunities for hurt feelings.

If Only It Weren't for You. In this game, the player explains why things are as they are and why he can do nothing about it. It is not really his fault, it is the fault of others — parents, teachers, society, and police. The real payoff, however, is that "it" never needs to consider any need for changing the one thing he can change – himself. He traps himself into making sure that nothing happens. Among pubescents and their parents, this game is often played as "If Only I Had a Honda."

Uproar. The classical game of Uproar is played between domineering fathers and teenage daughters. The end of the game is marked by anger, the slamming of doors, and running away – one solution to the threat of incest.

Poor Me. In this game, "it" invests a great deal of time in self-pity or self-depreciation. The game can be played in a number of styles, such as, "See How Hard I Try," "Ain't It Awful," or "Why Does This Always Happen to Me?" The answer to the latter question is usually, "Because that's how you set it up."

I'm Only Trying To Help. In this game, "it" gives people ineffective help they do not want or do not need. When they come back no better off, both players end up feeling helpless, hopeless, and exasperated.

Whatever the game, these transactions create a great deal of excitement and reinforce the basic stances that a person has taken toward himself and others. They also allow the players to avoid closeness and intimacy, sexual or otherwise.

IV. Script Analysis

At some point, every child decides two important questions: (1) "What kind of person am I?" and (2) "What happens to people like me?" We make these decisions on the basis of the information available to us, and our abilities to interpret it. Unfortunately, because of inexperience, the information or our interpretation of it may be inadequate, if not incorrect. It is, however, on such a basis that we answer these two great questions – and plan our lives accordingly. Such a life-plan, decided early in life under the influence of those who raised us and reaffirmed by later events, is our script (Berne, 1972; Steiner, 1974).

The most important messages that young children receive about themselves come from the significant authority figures in their lives. These messages take the form of expectations, approval and disapproval, encouragement and discouragement. They may be verbal or nonverbal. The messages come from what the child sees, from what he hears, and from what he feels.

The strongest negative messages young children receive are usually communicated at a feeling level. Since the negative part is often mixed with a more readily identifiable and verbal positive part, these messages may be very difficult to recognize. For example, when parents keep insisting again and again how much they really did want a baby girl, part of the message is actually that the child should not have been what she is: "You should have been a boy." "Don't be you."

The Gouldings (1976) have identified twelve constellations of such negative messages or injunctions.

1. Don't Be
2. Don't Be You
3. Don't Be Close
4. Don't Be Sane
5. Don't Make It
6. Don't

7. Don't Be a Child
8. Don't Be a Grownup
9. Don't Be Important
10. Don't Belong
11. Don't Think
12. Don't Feel

The more strongly these injunctions are given and the greater the survival value of the person who gives them, the more likely they will be incorporated into the child's decisions about himself. However, just because a child is given an injunction, he does not necessarily have to accept it. Some perversely refuse. Even if he does accept the injunction, he can make a wide range of decisions based on it. For example, the child who accepts the injunction

"Don't Make It" may decide: (1) "I never can be a success, but I'll try," (2) "I'll just give up now," (3) "I'll not do anything and make others do it for me," or (4) "I'll work hard at being a failure and really show them." Having decided "who he is" and "what is supposed to happen" to people like him, the child may then begin to screen and to interact with the world in such a way as to reaffirm these basic decisions. Thus, he sets up and maintains a series of self-fulfilling prophecies that reinforce his view of himself, others, and the world; and he begins to elicit, cultivate, and treasure the specific feelings he needs to maintain his stance.

Children get rewarded for the things which please adults. This is one way injunctions are enforced. For example, the child who is rewarded each time he is ineffective or incompetent learns how to please his parents—by failing. Similarly, other children learn that they get rewards for not being around, for not being demanding, and for not seeking attention; that is, the parents inadvertently reinforce the injunction "Don't Be."

People can play out their basic life-plan in a variety of currencies. They can "Not Make It" as a janitor, a penitentiary inmate, or even as the president of a bank. The particular currency in which they play depends in large measure on their parents' messages as to how to be a success. These messages, which are verbal and occur later in life than the injunctions, are known as counterinjunctions. Five of these counterinjunctions are especially destructive. They are all open-ended and consequently can lead to driven behavior (Kahler, 1974). They are similar to some of Ellis's "irrational beliefs" (see Chapter 4). Unfortunately, they are also frequently given out in the process of discipline. These are:

1. "Be Perfect." Since perfection is generally impossible for human beings, this is often an invitation to fail.

2. "Be Strong." Many children hear this as "Don't Feel."
3. "Hurry Up." It is difficult to know just how fast is "Up."
4. "Work Harder." How hard is "Hard"?
5. "Please Me." Since a person cannot please everyone, this is another invitation to fail. For many people, this becomes "Don't be you, be what others want," "Don't think what you think," or "Don't feel what you feel."

It is possible to bring this material together, to look at the forces that lead a young person to make the life-decisions that he does. The following case history indicates how this can be done.

Charles: A teenager in trouble. Charles, a sixteen-year-old with a colorful history of break-ins, police chases, gang fights, and newspaper headlines, was found unconscious in a shopping center, as a result of an overdose of barbiturates. His father, a prominent community businessman and politician, tried to hush up the boy's mother when she stated to the hospital nurses that she was sorry Charles had not killed himself and that he had been nothing but a nuisance all of his life.

When Charles regained consciousness, he stated that he felt guilty for existing because he could not live up to his father's expectations and that he had always felt there was no place for him. On his fifth birthday, when his parents had refused to give him a birthday party, Charles had decided that he would kill himself — in such a way as to show them up and punish them. Both Charles and his parents expected that he would end up badly, probably in prison, and that he would die young, certainly not older than twenty-one.

Charles's mother was not a villain or a crazy woman. In reality, she was a rather depressed, long-suffering person at her wit's end. She had found herself pregnant with Charles at a time when she was planning to divorce her husband because of his numerous infidelities and his alcoholism. It was against her religious beliefs to have an abortion. She had no education or vocational skills and was afraid to leave the marriage. Charles symbolized the blocks to having a better life, and because of his physical resemblance to his father, she often displaced her anger toward her husband onto him.

Charles's father, an intelligent and intellectual man, had once had high hopes for his son. These hopes were dashed when he discovered that Charles's intellectual level was only normal. At that point he decided that "at least Charles could look good." The father's unspoken — and consciously unintended — message was that since Charles could not "look good" through normal means, he should use extranormal means, such as drugs.

The psychological matrix out of which Charles decided, at age five, to "show them up, even if it kills me," can be diagrammed as shown on page 114.

BASIC ASSUMPTIONS AND CHARACTERISTICS OF TRANSACTIONAL ANALYSIS

Although different workers use transactional theory in different ways, depending upon their own personalities, the people with whom they work, and the context of their work, there are six major emphases which form a constellation distinguishing it from the other approaches in this book, although it may share one or two emphases with each of them.

1. *Man Is Basically OK.* Transactional Analysis can be classified with those approaches that look upon man as basically OK, or at least potentially so. This is not to be interpreted as some Pollyanna view that everyone is "nice" or that we necessarily like everyone or approve of

Charles: Decision for Drug Abuse

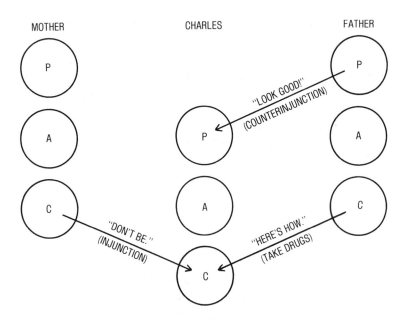

Injunction: Don't Be.
Counterinjunction: Look Good.
Decision: I'll show them up even if it kills me.
Game: Cops and Robbers.
Basic Existential Position: I'm not OK and neither are you.
Script Outcome: Suicide, probably in prison.

---

what they do. It does not mean that we do not see psychopathology in people or that we attribute problems in child rearing merely to ignorance.

Early in life, as we develop awareness of the differences between ourselves and others, we elaborate a basic position that defines us in relationship to others in the world. These positions can be generalized into:

a. I'm OK or I'm Not OK.
b. You're OK or You're Not OK.

Each of these positions can be experienced with varying degrees of intensity. Some people may feel totally "I'm OK," or "I'm Not OK"; however most people feel OK about some parts of themselves and not OK about other parts (for instance, a person may feel confident and competent about himself at work, but not in his sexual role). People often switch into different positions in different situations, but over a period of time they spend a majority of their time in one of them — their basic existential position. On the basis of these positions, we meet others and set up interactional systems wherein certain specific transactions are possible and others are not. In Transactional Analysis, we look upon the position "I'm OK and So Are You" as man's basic natural stance; deviations from it are seen as manifestations of pathology.

Each of these positions contains a program for what to do about solving problems, including those of child rearing and of discipline. In the "I'm OK, You Are Not" position, a person often thinks, "If there is any problem here, it is your fault and we can solve the problem by getting rid of you." In the "I'm Not OK, You Are" position, he is likely to think, "Whatever is wrong has happened because I'm sick, bad, or stupid, and I should leave." In the "I'm Not OK, and Neither Are You" position, a person feels hopeless and gets nowhere. Only the "I'm OK, and So Are You" position is effective in solving problems and in long-term personal relationships.

The basic stance "I'm OK, You Are Not" or "I'm Not OK, You Are" sets the stage for competition and a pseudo-win/lose situation. Interactions are seen in terms of winning and losing, of getting or of being got. The emphasis of transactions of this kind involves self-esteem; solving problems at hand may be neglected. In reality, over the long term both parties lose.

Disciplining needs to be done from the position, "I'm OK, and So Are You." The child may need to behave differently to solve problems. He does not need to be made not OK! It is his actions which are unacceptable, not him or his internal experiences.

2. *The Importance of Stroking.* An attractive twenty-year-old woman brought her four-month-old baby to the local guidance center, at the insistence of her pediatrician. The pediatrician could find no physical cause for the child at four months to weigh two pounds less than it had at birth.

The clinic's social worker noticed that when the young woman came in, she placed the child in the corner of the room and then never looked at it again during the entire interview. The give-and-take between mother and child that seems so typical of mothers and their babies at this age was entirely absent. Suspecting that the child was not held enough, not stroked enough, not rocked enough, the social worker advised the mother to spend about ten minutes each hour during the day holding and rocking the child, and made an appointment for her to come back the following day. The following week the young mother phoned, stating that the pediatrician had told her to come back to the clinic; however, she did not want to come, because she had done what the social worker had suggested once — and it had not worked. The following day the baby died.

One of our basic needs is for stimulation from outside ourselves. Adequate physical stroking and touch is particularly important in the survival and growth of infants. As we grow older, we can also accept other strokes: a smile or a look, words of praise or of punishment. We also learn how to stroke ourselves and how to use internal stroking as a reward.

Stroking not only ensures our survival, it also is used as a reward to help us learn things and to maintain social patterns. We all learn ways to give and get strokes in the families in which we were raised. Unless we make specific efforts to change our preferences and our behavior, the kind of strokes we become accustomed to as children are the kind we seek from others throughout our lives.

There are four types of strokes.
a. Positive strokes, such as a hug or praise
b. Negative strokes, such as a slap or rebuke
c. Conditional strokes; that is, strokes for doing
d. Unconditional strokes; that is, strokes for being
This typology can be summarized as follows:

A Stroke Typology

	Conditional Strokes	Unconditional Strokes
Positive Strokes	Rewards	Love just for existing
Negative Strokes	Punishment	Anger, rejection just for existing

In some families, most strokes are negative. At worst, the child may be hit just for existing, an unconditional negative stroke. More commonly, the child is disregarded unless he gets into trouble, a negative conditional stroke. Such children learn to be negative and destructive in order to gain some strokes, for negative strokes are better than none at all. As adults, they are likely to continue to seek negative strokes and to ignore or distrust any positive ones.

Behavior which is stroked will be repeated. A child who receives mainly unconditional strokes, whether positive or negative, is not likely to respond to the demands of school and will appear unmotivated to his teachers. In contrast, a child from an achievement-oriented family, who receives only positive conditional strokes for learning, learns that he must perform and produce. He grows up feeling unstroked, empty, and unlovable if he is not achieving. For optimal growth, people need both conditional and unconditional strokes, and a vast preponderance of the positive over the negative. It is important, however, that the positive stroking be for behavior the parent wants to encourage. Most of what has traditionally been called discipline has involved conditional negative strokes. The child is stroked, albeit negatively, for his misbehavior. Laymen say, "He did it just to get attention."

A major task for the parent or the teacher is to help the child get more positive strokes. Unfortunately, if a child is raised on negative strokes, he may come to distrust and ignore the positive ones. He will have to relearn how to take positive ones before we can expect him to give up the negative ones. To give up the negative ones without being able to take positive ones is to have to exist with none at all.

The astute student will probably have recognized that under the term "stroking," the transactional analyst may utilize any of the behavior modification strategies described by Dr. Madsen and Dr. Stephens (see Chapter 7). Learning theorists speak of contingencies and rewards; transactional analysts speak of strokes. Learning theorists emphasize changing or maintaining behavior patterns; transactional analysts emphasize the importance of strokes for feeling good, and for life itself.

3. *People Have Options.* Most of the time, we tend to respond automatically in old patterns of behavior and do not realize that there may be a number of responses open to us. Transactional analysts put a great deal of emphasis on the individual becoming aware of his options. We have options in how we hear and in how we respond. The framework of structural analysis provides a useful

means of looking at these options.

4. *Responsibility for Feelings.* A common myth is that we have no control over our feelings, but that others do. However, if one accepts the idea that we have options concerning how we hear things and how we respond, then it follows that we also have considerable control over our feelings. Consequently, we are not entitled to project the responsibility for them onto others.

With the exception of grief and mourning, which are reparative and necessary processes and of momentary frustration, most feelings generally regarded as negative —anger, anxiety, confusion, sadness, etc.—are highly suspect to the transactional analyst. If they are habitual or chronic, they are likely being cultivated to reinforce our existential positions or our basic script decisions. Such feelings we term "rackets," and regard as pathological.

If an individual takes responsibility for his feelings, then he takes responsibility for not liking what another person does or says. He may say something like "I feel angry when the boss scolds me like a child." However, he is not entitled to say "The boss *makes* me angry when he scolds me like a child." In the area of child rearing, we can certainly empathize with a woman who feels angry at her children, but she is very different from the woman who says and indeed believes, "My children *make* me angry."

5. *The Importance of Multileveled Messages.* Many messages may be given at the same time. At the very least, there are usually (a) an overt informational message, (b) a relationship message, and (c) some kind of meta-communication about how the other messages are to be understood. For example, you may have walked down the hall and said "Hi! How are you?" to someone and expected them to reply, "Fine, how are you?" However, if

they misunderstood your metamessage, they may actually have told you how they felt — much to your discomfort.

In transactional analysis, we put considerable emphasis on looking at messages which may be out of the sender's awareness. It is not just that people lack information about how to behave. They may behave in ways that are destructive, but that make good sense to their Child, and of which the rest of them (Parent and Adult) is unaware.

Example: Each time Dorothy, a developing sixteen-year-old, went out with a boyfriend, her father lectured her on what not to let her boyfriend do. On her return, he excitedly demanded a minute description of her activities of the evening.

Dorothy had three illegitimate children.

On the one hand, father told Dorothy not to have intercourse. This is a message from his Parent, and the message of which he was aware. However, his smile, the excited gleam in his eyes and his excessive attention to the subject gave her a very different message, a message from his Child. This second message was the more powerful, yet it was one out of his awareness. Indeed, this second message was probably the last thing he would consciously have wished to send. These messages may be diagrammed as shown on page 121.

Prohibitions beginning with "Don't" may act as a guidebook. However the parent or teacher may intend them, such statements really tell the youngster more or less what he is expected to do, if he has not already thought of it. Sometimes, these messages are only the verbal part of a double message. The other side, outside the sender's awareness, conveys his excitement or his gratification with the misbehavior.

6. *Permission.* Each individual needs a number of very specific permissions in order to grow and to develop into

Dorothy: Programming for "Unwanted" Pregnancy

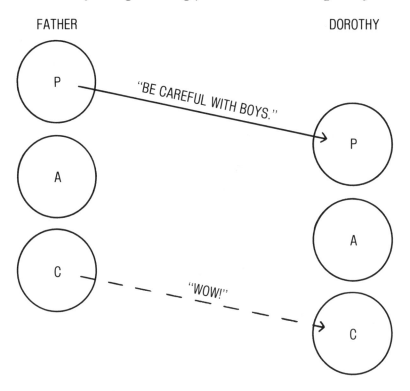

a full and integrated human being. Originally these permissions should come from those who raise us; ultimately each of us must give them to himself (Allen, J. R., and Allen, 1972).

Each permission seems important throughout the life cycle, but each gains major importance during a certain period. To some extent, each new level depends on a successful acceptance and integration of the previous ones. This hierarchy of permissions may be outlined as follows:

a. Permission to be; this level has two major aspects

    i. Permission to be alive, to breathe, to occupy space, to exist

    ii. Permission to live with zest

b. Permission to be aware of one's own experiences and sensations, and a little later, of one's own thoughts

c. Permission to be emotionally close, yet remain a separate individual — that is, to avoid symbiosis

d. Permission to be oneself, of appropriate age and sex

e. Permission to be aware of one's basic stance toward oneself, others, and the world

f. Permission to change and grow in an atmosphere of feedback, support, and trust

g. Permission to be OK, while allowing others to be OK and acknowledging the importance of the context

h. Permission to think clearly and to solve problems effectively

i. Permission to "make it" in love and work, and to be important

j. Permission to find or make some meaning of existence

This progression of permissions fits with Erikson's assumptions that the human personality develops according to steps which are predetermined by the individual's readiness to be aware of and to interaction with a widening social radius and that society (at least in principle) tends to invite and meet this succession of potentialities and encourages the optimal rate and sequence of their unfolding. It also implies that all these levels of permission — and their corresponding psychosocial strengths — are interrelated and that each level exists in some form before its critical time arrives.

    The importance of these permissions at different parts of the life cycle, as well as at their critical time, has led to considerable interest in developmental psychology. This will be dealt with in a later section.

GOALS OF TRANSACTIONAL ANALYSIS

The goals of transactional analysis are that the individual be in charge of his life, function autonomously, exercise his options with responsibility and spontaneity, and that he integrate the ten permissions which we have outlined. We would expect him to spend most of his time in the basic stance "I'm OK, You're OK" (and the context counts); to have committed himself fully to a life of vigor and zest; to be aware of his own experience, sensations and thoughts; to be himself; to be capable of warm closeness; to be aware of his basic stance toward himself and others; to be free to change; to be able to think clearly and solve problems effectively; to "make it" in love and work; and to find some meaning in existence. These are also our standards for decisions in child rearing and, consequently, in discipline.

TRANSACTIONAL ANALYSIS AND DISCIPLINE

All the contributors to this book will probably emphasize that the term discipline has many meanings. In a broad sense, it refers to training people to act in accordance with some standard of proper conduct. It is related to the word *disciple*. The term is also used to refer to immediate behavior in the handling of misconduct. This use of the word has to lead to the equation of the term with punishment or penalization.

There are no formal rules for TA discipline. There are no formal techniques which are specifically connected with transactional analysis. In reality, we might use techniques that were developed by any group or we might create them on the spur of the moment, provided they fit for the person who is disciplining, the child, and the context in which the disciplining is done. However, as has been depicted under the goals of transactional analysis, we do have a general model which is a kind of ideal toward which we would like to encourage our children to grow.

In looking at discipline, the transactional analyst will likely put much attention on two questions. These are:

1. How is this disciplining behavior to be done and how will the child experience this:
   a. From the framework of structural analysis?
   b. From the framework of existential positions?
   c. From the framework of transactional and game analysis?
   d. From the viewpoint of script analysis?
      i. What messages are given to the child (e.g., injunctions, counterinjunctions)?
      ii. What kind of child do the parenting people need to create in order to meet their own script needs?
2. Is this the disciplinary behavior appropriate to this child, at this age, at this time, in this context:
   a. From the viewpoint of the child's level of intellectual development?
   b. From the viewpoint of the child's level of emotional development?

Many parents and teachers who read books on child rearing discover to their horror that the technique which looks so good on paper and which apparently works so well in the next house or classroom is ineffective, or perhaps even destructive, in their hands. From the transactional point of view, it is very important to look at *how* any technique is used, for the manner of its use may often be much more important than the technique. We have found that the frameworks of TA are useful in doing this.

I. Disciplining as Analyzed from the Framework of Structural Analysis

The parent ego-state may be manifest in two func-

tional entities:
1. The Nurturant Parent ego-state
2. The Critical Parent ego-state
In the basic structural analysis diagram, these functional entities are diagrammed as shown on page 126.

The positive aspects of the Nurturant Parent ego-state include permission-giving, and appropriate nurturance. In its negative aspect, this becomes the inappropriate nurturance of "smothering."

The positive aspects of the Critical Parent ego-state include protection and standard definition. In its negative aspect, this becomes inappropriate criticism and harassment. It is this aspect that we consider responsible for guilt and self-torture. The individual berates himself with a barrage of "You should have," "Why didn't you?" messages that tell him he is sick, bad, stupid, or crazy.

Some find it easier to parent from their Nurturant Parent. Others, and especially those whose early life included little warm parenting, may find it safer and easier to parent from their Adult. However, with some effort, they can learn to develop their own Nurturant Parent. Many parents do not begin soon enough to try to reach their children's own Adult, to give them permission to think, and to help them solve problems.

Roughly in order of effectiveness, we do parenting or disciplining from Nurturant Parent, Critical Parent, Adult, or Child. Depending on the circumstances, any of these may be appropriate.

II. Disciplining as Analyzed from the Framework of Transactional Analysis

Four types of transactions between children and their parents or teachers are of special importance in discipline: Nurturant- or Critical-Parent-to-Child, Adult-to-Adult, and Child-to-Child. Each is outlined and diagrammed on the following pages.

Functional Analysis

CRITICAL PARENT

CP

NP   NURTURANT PARENT

A_2

C_2

1. *The Nurturant-Parent-to-Child Transaction.* This type of transaction is one of permission and care. It may be enough in itself, or it may be used to calm a frightened, unhappy Child, as a prelude to an Adult-to-Adult transaction. This sequence fosters appropriate overt behavior, the learning of cause-and-effect relationships, and the consideration of alternatives; that is, it encourages Adult functioning.

2. *The Critical-Parent-to-Child Transaction.* This type of transaction is useful and powerful in stopping the child from doing things which may be dangerous. At its best, it is a transaction of firm limit-setting and of protection. It is usually best followed by transactions of the Adult-

The Nurturant-Parent-to-Child Transaction

PARENT CHILD

NP P

A A

"YOU DON'T HAVE TO MISBEHAVE TO GET ATTENTION!"

C C

The Critical-Parent-to-Child Transaction

PARENT CHILD

NP
CP P

A A

"DON'T!"

C C

to-Adult type. At its worst, such transactions may lead the child into being afraid and angry. This can interfere with his learning; indeed, he may learn to escape, to avoid, to accuse or to hit as methods of problem solving.

3. *The Adult-to-Adult Transaction.* This is a transaction of reasoned judgment and of rationality. It leads to a consideration of options and alternatives, of outcomes and consequences in an objective and unemotional manner. However, when a child is angry or upset, this transaction is unlikely to be useful, unless a Nurturant-Parent-to-Child transaction precedes it. In other circumstances, it is often most useful for the parenting person to go directly into his Adult, and to attempt to reach the child's Adult.

The Adult-to-Adult transaction is not possible until the child has a functioning Adult, about age two. Parents often underestimate the ease with which they can reach a child's Adult. In older children, adolescents, and grown-ups, this transaction can lead to a redefinition of goals, a description of observable behavior to be changed, and to the nonemotional establishment of a system of rewards — including self-stroking, in which a person can become his own "behavior mod" therapist!

4. *The Child-to-Child Transaction.* In constrast to the above transactions, discipline from a Child ego-state is very different. Often it is based on the parenting person's jealousy or guilt. Essentially, it represents one young child trying to parent another. It is generally highly emotional, erratic, and ineffectual. For example, child-abuse may develop when a mother's Child ego-state is desperate, upset, and wants her infant son to love her. She needs to energize her Adult ego-state to figure out how to take care of her son when he cries and to energize her Parent ego-state to soothe him. Instead, in her Child ego-state she may expect the infant to take care of her.

The Adult-to-Adult Transaction

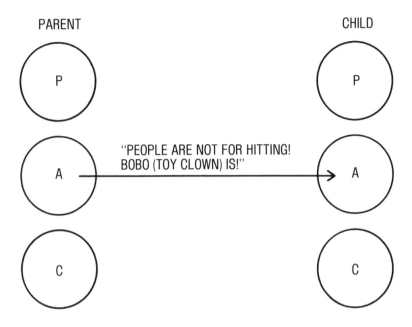

PARENT   CHILD

P   P

A   →   "PEOPLE ARE NOT FOR HITTING!   A
          BOBO (TOY CLOWN) IS!"

C   C

If the infant does not parent her, she may punish him for being defiant, ungrateful, or unloving. Such pathogenic parenting may be diagrammed as shown on page 130.

It is ideal when parents can relate to their children from all ego-states. It is a delight to see parents enter into joyous Child-to-Child reciprocity with their infant. However, it is important that these parents can also cathect, when appropriate, their Adults and their Parents.

Drama Triangle. Another way of looking at disciplining transactions comes from the framework of the Drama Triangle. For good drama, one needs a victim. However, it is very difficult to be a victim all by oneself; to play the role properly, one needs someone to provide either perse-

Pathogenic Parenting

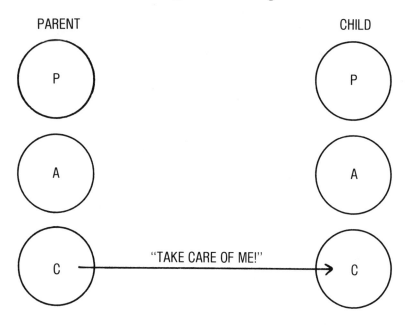

PARENT   CHILD

"TAKE CARE OF ME!"

cution or a rescue. Similarly, it is very difficult to be a Persecutor or a Rescuer without a Victim. These three roles—Victim, Persecutor, and Rescuer—form the Drama Triangle. Each player takes a prescribed role for a while, and then the players switch. Let us consider a discipline problem from this viewpoint.

Example: Sue, age fifteen, comes home at 3:00 A.M. Her mother asks, "Where were you? We were worried sick!"

Sue replies, "It's my life and my business!"

The father, who has entered the room by this time, shouts, "Don't you dare speak to your mother that way!" and hits her, despite the mother's efforts to calm him down. Sue runs out of the house, screaming that she will "never, never return."

These transactions can be analyzed on the drama triangle as shown on pages 132 and 133. When in the Drama Triangle, people do not think clearly or solve problems effectively. This type of interaction makes for great excitement, many strokes, lots of feeling — and lousy living.

A person who is disciplining may act as a Rescuer or Persecutor and function from the existential position "I'm OK, You Are Not." The Victim acts from "I'm Not OK, You Are" or "I'm Not OK, and Neither Are You (and I'll rub your nose in it)." Acceptable disciplining is very unlikely to be done by people caught up in the Drama Triangle.

There is such a thing as true help as opposed to Drama Triangle rescue, and it is important that discipline be a form of true help, not a Drama Triangle rescue. Some of the major differences may be summarized as follows:

Person Giving Real Help	*Person Involved in Drama Triangle Rescuing*
1. Stays in "I'm OK, You're OK and the context counts"	1. Usually operates from "I'm OK, You Are Not"
2. Much Adult functioning	2. Little Adult functioning
3. Responds to request	3. Offers unrequested help
4. Makes offer and makes clear contract	4. Does not find out if the offer is wanted, and does not make a clear contract
5. Gives what is needed and only as long as it is needed (Adult)	5. Does not give appropriately
6. Seeks ongoing feedback (Adult)	6. Does not seek feedback
7. Checks outcome (Adult)	7. Does not check outcome
8. The helper's identity and self-esteem do not depend on his being a helper; he does not feel bad if turned down	8. Identity and self-esteem are at risk; the outcome *per se* is of secondary importance

Drama Triangle

DRAMA TRIANGLE: TIME 1

RESCUER: MOTHER
  "WHERE WERE YOU? WE
WERE WORRIED SICK!"

PERSECUTOR

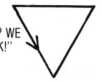

VICTIM:
(SUE COMES IN LATE)

DRAMA TRIANGLE: TIME 2

RESCUER

PERSECUTOR: SUE
  "IT'S MY LIFE
AND MY BUSINESS!"

VICTIM:
MOTHER

DRAMA TRIANGLE: TIME 3

RESCUER

PERSECUTOR:
MOTHER

VICTIM: SUE
"YOU DON'T TRUST ME!"

DRAMA TRIANGLE: TIME 4

RESCUER: FATHER
  "DON'T TALK TO YOUR
MOTHER THAT WAY!"

PERSECUTOR:
SUE

VICTIM:
MOTHER

DRAMA TRIANGLE: TIME 5

RESCUER: MOTHER
"NOW DEAR!"

PERSECUTOR:
FATHER

VICTIM:
SUE

DRAMA TRIANGLE: TIME 6

RESCUER

PERSECUTOR:
(FATHER SLAPS
SUE)

VICTIM:
SUE

DRAMA TRIANGLE: TIME 7

RESCUER

PERSECUTOR: SUE
"I'LL NEVER
COME BACK!"

VICTIM:
FATHER AND MOTHER

*III. Discipline Analyzed from the Framework of the
Existential Position*

A third way of looking at how parenting is done is
from the framework of existential positions. It is important that the parenting person let himself count and be
OK, that he let the child count and be OK, and that he
also count the context in which the parenting is done.

Any disciplining technique can be utilized in such a
way to convey the message that the child is not OK. It is
important to look not at the words that the parenting figure uses, but rather at his style of interaction. It is important to look at what happens to those with less power,
namely the child. Are his or her hopes, wishes, fears, and
expectations taken into consideration, or did all consideration go only to the hopes, fears, wishes, expectations,
and convenience of the parenting figure?

If disciplining is done from the stance that the parent
or teacher is OK and counts and the child does not, or
vice-versa, then the child learns to see life in terms of
winning or losing, of getting or being got. He may shape
up for the moment, but it is at a high cost.

*IV. Discipline Analyzed from the Framework of
Script Analysis*

1. The Child's Script. One of the important issues in
looking at any disciplining technique from a TA point of
view is what sort of messages the child will get from this
procedure. What are the injunctions he will receive and
what messages will he get about his OKness?

A major aspect of this analysis is looking at the things
for which the child is stroked. What is stroked will be repeated. This is one way that injunctions are reinforced.
For example, some children get rewarded each time they
fail. This reinforces the injunction "Don't make it" or
"Don't grow up"—probably the very last thing his par-

ents or teachers would consciously wish to do.

A frequent mistake in parenting arises when children are not given enough "What to do" messages (Nurturant Parent and Adult). Almost inevitably, children incorporate many "Don't!" messages, but may lack a capacity to use these messages if they do not have options for acceptable behavior. However, verbal "shoulds" only provide a setup for children to feel not-OK if they are unable to accomplish them or have no alternates.

2. *The Parents' Scripts.* Scripts function to maintain our psychosocial status quo. They are analogous to those physiological processes which maintain our blood sugar, temperature, and pulse-rate within that relatively narrow range which is compatible with life. Because a person acts within his script, he will choose the kind of long-term relationship — such as that with spouse or employer — which fits with the needs of his script.

As parents, we raise the children we need. If one is to be another King Lear, he needs to start training his children early, so that they will play the parts well. It is because we train our children to meet our script needs without being aware of it that we may end up giving them messages which consciously we would abhor.

Example: Mrs. Jones was a matronly, well-preserved, energetic, and intelligent woman of sixty-five. She had decided early in life that it was her role to "work her fingers to the bone" to hold her family together and that she would receive no appreciation whatsoever for this care. She also had decided to be strong and to bear up valiantly.

As a young woman, she married a doctor who was — and who remained — addicted to barbiturates. She managed to nurse him through numerous bouts of withdrawal and to keep the secret of his addiction from the professional community. They had one child, a girl she decided was "frail." Mrs. Jones attempted to tell this girl what she (the child) thought and felt, discounting the girl's own thoughts and feelings, "because you are too young to know what you really want," even when the "child" was herself a middle-aged mother.

At Mrs. Jones' insistence, the daughter married a very wealthy and promising young man. After the marriage, Mrs. Jones would phone as often as nine or ten times per day to make sure her daughter was "all right." When the daughter objected, Mrs. Jones interpreted this as more evidence that her daughter was frail and would phone back once again to make sure there wasn't anything she could do to be of help.

At Christmas time, in order to make sure that she could buy the daughter a present that the daughter would really like, Mrs. Jones hit upon the following plan. Her daughter was to go to a local craft store and choose five or six articles which she particularly liked and was to tell the proprietor of her choices. Mrs. Jones would then go to the same store and choose one of the five or six items as a present. Thus, her daughter would receive a present she wished, but yet something which would also be a surprise.

On viewing her daughter's selections, Mrs. Jones announced that her daughter didn't really want any of those presents, and chose an entirely different one. The following day her daughter had a psychotic break, marked by an inability to know what she thought, what she felt, or what she wanted.

In looking at this brief case history, we could say that the daughter received the injunctions "Don't think," "Don't be honest with your feelings," "Don't grow up." However, from the viewpoint of mother's script, the daughter had really been trained to fit in with mother's pattern of "working her fingers to the bone" in her unappreciated efforts to take care of others. Indeed, as the daughter recovered from her schizophrenic break, Dr. Jones "took to bed" because of depression.

While this history may strike some readers as smacking too much of gross psychopathology, these same processes are operative in us all. In gross psychopathology, they are merely written in large letters. Sometimes the parent who says, "This child will be the death of me" is planning just that.

From the transactional point of view, it is most important that we do not discipline our children into meeting the needs of our scripts, but rather give them the permissions and protection they need to be able to develop their lives spontaneously, creatively, and responsibly.

THE APPROPRIATENESS OF DISCIPLINE TECHNIQUES

From the viewpoint of transactional analysis, it is important that discipline techniques be appropriate for the specific child in question. It is important that any technique fit the child's level of intellectual development and his level of emotional development and that it incorporate appropriate permission and protection for this child, at this stage, in his particular context.

Many problems of discipline are really problems associated with finding techniques appropriate to a child's particular stage of development. Many "behavior problems" are really the manifestations of unresolved developmental tasks of an earlier stage.

Children develop through a series of stages, each with its own tasks and each leaving its own residues (Leven, 1974; Schiff, 1975). The goal of parenting is to rear a healthy child to independence and maturity. This involves the formulation of a healthy symbiosis followed by its resolution at a rate consistent with biological and social demands. Early in life, parenting figures function as the infant's Adult and Parent. However, as the children grow up, they themselves must take responsibility for making themselves do the "right" thing and for testing-out doing the "wrong" ones. Parents need to be sufficiently flexible to permit this and yet respond with the appropriate conditional stroking.

DEVELOPMENTAL STAGES AND SECONDARY STRUCTURAL ANALYSIS

In the following section, we will sketch, albeit incompletely, the development of the personality through a series of stages. Each stage is associated with the addition of a new personality structure, and at each stage the child has special needs. This framework is known as secondary structural analysis. It does not translate easily into the functional analysis of personality that we have previously described. This developmental framework is also not unique to TA. The student will undoubtedly notice much that has been drawn from Freud, Erikson, Piaget, their followers, and their detractors.

The First Six Months

This is the period when the infant discovers he exists. The parental tasks are to think for the baby and to figure out what he needs (Adult), to nurture him appropriately and to supply unconditional positive strokes (Nurturant Parent). It is not possible to spoil a baby with unconditional positive strokes, but it is possible to be so overresponsive that the child does not learn to put out minimal energy in getting his needs met.

Babies need to become increasingly more aware of their needs, to do something to get their needs met, and to be rewarded for their efforts. The sequence, "need (pain or hunger) → action (cry) → response (strokes or food) → pleasure," is crucial. It seems to be a major step in the child's learning to think. It is the initial step in the development of initiative and activity in getting needs met. It is a source for decisions as to whether to trust the world.

When his behavior does not produce appropriate results, the child is likely to increase his activity. This may lay the foundation for later agitation rather than effective problem-solving. Alternatively, he may try substitute behaviors. This may lay the foundations for later pathology.

Structurally, at this stage it is mother's Adult ego-state which does the thinking and problem-solving for both of them, and her Parent ego-state which defines what is important. Her Child ego-state may merge with the baby's, creating a symbiosis. The infant's personality structure may be diagrammed as shown on page 140.

Mid-Infancy: 6–18 Months

At this stage, children become mobile and develop control over their bodies; consequently they become more independent. For some parents this period of increasing mobility and independence may not be appealing, especially as the child drools and smears.

About twelve to fifteen months, the child more actively explores other things in his environment; it is a period of increased curiosity, exploration and learning, of seeking more strokes, excitement, and varied experiences. At this stage good parenting includes providing a safe environment and opportunities for the child to experiment and explore. It is only at this stage that conditional, as well as unconditional, strokes become important. Whenever possible they should be positive and for appropriate behavior.

Structurally, at this stage we see the beginning of the Adult in the Child ego-state, the Little Professor, as diagrammed on page 141.

Personality Structure: 0–6 Months

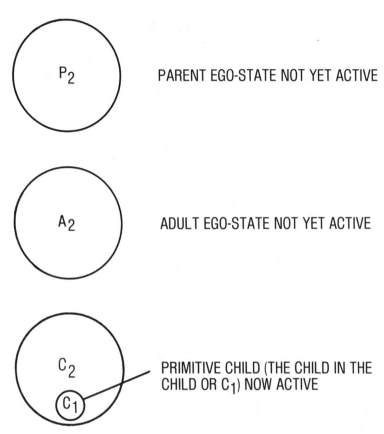

PARENT EGO-STATE NOT YET ACTIVE

ADULT EGO-STATE NOT YET ACTIVE

PRIMITIVE CHILD (THE CHILD IN THE CHILD OR C_1) NOW ACTIVE

Separation Stage: 18 Months–3 Years

The "terrible twos" are a period when the infant learns that the world does not revolve around him and that others also have feelings and wants. This leads to anger, sulking, and temper outburst. It is important that the parents still offer the protection of their care, yet help the

Personality Structure: 6–18 Months

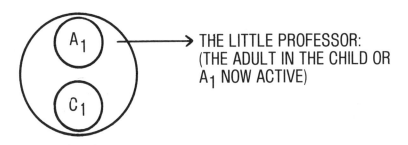

THE LITTLE PROFESSOR:
(THE ADULT IN THE CHILD OR
A_1 NOW ACTIVE)

child experience the necessity of social conformity.

The parents may encourage the child to act out his rebelliousness, may make demands too early so the child does not completely experience the conflict, or may make too few demands. This can leave residues of negativism or overcompliance or the angry discounting of anyone who might cause a person to think they are not the center of the universe.

It is at this stage that the symbiosis between the child and mother begins to break up. While some theorists have emphasized temper tantrums as evidence of emerging individuality, transactional workers also take into account the opposite view. Much negativistic behavior is really an effort to have someone else think for or take care of one; that is, it functions to maintain the symbiosis. When the child resolves the task of separating and begins to think autonomously, he is ready for the next stage. However, beginning thinkers who behave quite intelligently around others may not think so well around those with whom they are in symbiosis. They may push the limits so that parents call a halt. These transactions really push the parents to insist that the children start to think.

Toilet training may be the issue about which these wars are waged. However, if toilet training is not especially important to the parents, the battle will be fought in other areas. A parent who is caught up in a way of thinking that implies that a person who wins does so only at the expense of another is apt to pass this on. His child learns that all important events are win/lose situations.

Since toddlers have the ability to get into everything, it is tempting to shout "Don't!" This is inhibiting. It is better to say what he can do. Another characteristic of this stage is that children normally can take over responsibilities for going to sleep and for keeping themselves clean and dry.

The sullen two-year-old emerges into the trusting three, the spontaneous youngster who is clearly an individual child, no longer an infant. Structurally, his Adult (A_2) is now functioning (see diagram, page 143).

The Imagination Stage: 3–6 Years

These are years full of magical thinking and of expanding imagination. During this stage children form rough drafts of their scripts, decide their basic stance toward others, identify themselves sexually, and learn their roles in society. They may also experiment with expressing various feelings — such as well-staged temper tantrums — to see what happens. At this stage, children need many OK messages about sex, social roles, and an environment where they and others can be OK.

Children now learn how to scare themselves into conformity and good behavior, with scary thoughts and scary dreams. Transactional analysis has suggested that the child develops a Punitive Parent in his Child ego-state (P_1). He incorporates many messages into this Punitive Parent, frequently with extreme rigidity. It functions to provide internal controls, especially in those children

Personality Structure: 18 Months–3 Years

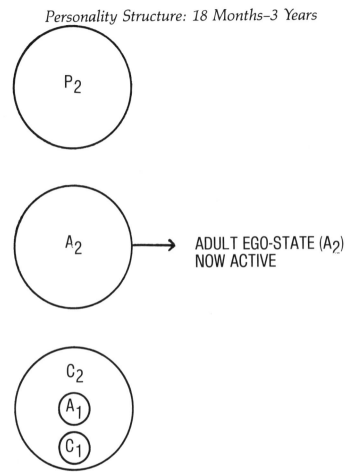

ADULT EGO-STATE (A$_2$)
NOW ACTIVE

who experience the external controls and protection as inadequate. This combination of fantasy and fear can also be used to elicit comfort and stroking from others (see diagram, page 144).

The Creative Activity Stage: 6–12 Years

Parents may find this an argumentative period—a period when the child actively challenges parental values

Personality Structure: Imagination Stage, 3–6 Years

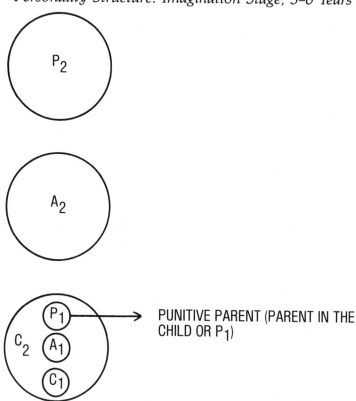

PUNITIVE PARENT (PARENT IN THE CHILD OR P_1)

—and very aggravating. The child is experimenting and developing his own internal value system. He may spend lots of time making others—especially those of the opposite sex—not OK.

It is important for the parents to stay involved and make ongoing demands for conformity. This is a time for parents to teach the functions of rules and techniques for settling disputes and to define clearly nonnegotiable demands and areas of freedom.

This is a period of activity, of seeking parenting from

others in the community, of competition, and of learning skills. The child learns to separate reality from fantasy (and hence knows what a lie is) and develops Adult ego-state cognitive functions and skills. Toward the end of this period the Parent ego-state (P_2) is cathectable. At this point, the child can be encouraged to consider problems from a value orientation and with a high degree of empathy; he can be expected to parent and look after himself, as well as smaller children (see diagram, page 146).

Adolescence

During this stage, the young person recycles all previous stages of development, broadening and deepening previous resolutions. Sometimes parents need to adapt from hour to hour, responding to the needs of a person who is "thirteen, going on one" or "thirteen, going on twenty-one." The final resolution of the symbiosis may be difficult for the parents as well as the child, and those who sense their parents' ambivalence or who are themselves ambivalent about leaving may set up situations so they get pushed out.

SUMMARY

Children do not come into the world exactly the same. Follow-up studies of infants clearly show that behavior traits such as activity level, rhythmicity, adaptability, and distractibility are fairly constant through early childhood and perhaps through life. These individual differences, apparently inborn and certainly evident in the first few weeks of life, preclude teaching children by any formula. By not taking into account their child's basic psychological nature — that is, by not letting the child be OK and not counting the congenital temperamental characteristics of this particular child — parents may unintentionally intensify characteristics they consider undesir-

Personality Structure: Creative Activity Stage, 6–12 Years

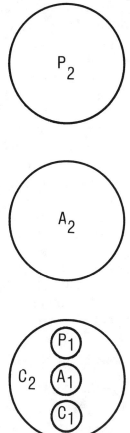

able and that might otherwise have been fleeting.

Children do not necessarily reach developmental stages at exactly the same time. Some reach them more quickly, others are much slower; and the parent needs to use his Adult to decide, often with the child, what would be best for the child at this time, in this particular setting.

This, then, is the view of the discipline of one couple, parents and transactional analysts. Depending on their own personalities, the children they have worked with, and the nature of their own children, other transactional analysts might emphasize slightly different aspects of TA Theory. However, all transactional analysts would probably emphasize how the disciplining behavior is to be done, how this child at this particular stage of development will experience the transaction, and what views the transaction may reinforce.

It is ideal when parents can relate to their children from all ego-states, from a stance of "I'm OK, You're OK, and the Context Counts," in a manner that is game-free, rich in positive strokes, and provided with the warmth of appropriate permissions and protection. Their children can grow up zestful, confident in their own basic OKness and the OKness of others, and free to actualize their potentialities for the benefit both of themselves and of society.

REFERENCES

Allen, J. G. (1973), Existential position and adjustment in a college population. *Transact. Anal. J.*, 3(4):22–25.

_____ and Webb, D. (1975), Stroking, existential position and mood in college students. *Transact. Anal. J.*, 5(3):227– 230.

Allen, J. R., and Allen, B. A. (1972), Scripts: The role of permission. *Transact. Anal. J.*, 2(2):72–74.

_____ and _____ (1978), *A Practitioner's Guide to Psychiatric Disorders.* Garden City, N.Y.: Medical Examination Publishing.

_____ and _____ (1977), Transactional paradigms of conflicts. In: *Current Issues in Transactional Analysis*, ed. R. Blakeney. New York: Brunner-Mazel.

Berne, E. (1964), *Games People Play.* New York: Grove Press.

_____ (1972), *What Do You Say After You Say Hello.* New York: Bantam.

Goulding, R., and Goulding, M. (1976), Injunctions, decisions and redecisions. *Transact. Anal. J.*, 6(1):41–48.

Jongeward, D., Ed. (1973), *Everybody Wins: Transactional Analysis Applied to Organizations*. Reading, Mass.: Addison-Wesley.

Kahler, T. (1974), Miniscript. *Transact. Anal. J.*, 4(1):26–42.

Leven, P. (1974), *Becoming the Way We Are*. Berkeley, Calif.: Privately published, P. O. Box 292.

Lieberman, M. A., Yalom, I. D., and Miles, M. B. (1973), *Encounter Groups: First Facts*. New York: Basic Books.

McCormick, P. (1973), TA and behavior modification: A comparison study. *Transact. Anal. J.*, 5(3):152–158.

Price, A. D. (1975), A paper and pencil instrument to measure ego-states. *Transact. Anal. J.*, 5(3):242–246.

Schiff, J., Ed. (1975), *Cathexis Reader: Transactional Analysis Treatment of Psychosis*. New York: Harper and Row.

Steiner, C. (1974), *Scripts People Live*. New York: Grove Press.

Thomas, A., Chess, S., and Birch, H. G. (1968), *Temperamental and Behavior Disorders in Children*. New York: New York University Press.

RECOMMENDED READINGS

Introductory

M. James and D. Jongeward. *Born to Win*. Reading, Mass.: Addison-Wesley, 1971.

P. McCormick and L. Campos. *Introduce Yourself to TA*. San Francisco, Cal.: Transactional Publishers.

C. Steiner. *Scripts People Live*. New York: Grove Press, 1974.

S. Woolams, M. Brown, and K. Huige. *Transactional Analysis in Brief*. Huron Valley Institute, 3443 Daleview, Ann Arbor, Mich. 48103.

Advanced

R. Blakeney, Ed. *Current Issues in Transactional Analysis: Proceedings of the First European Conference*. New York: Brunner-Mazel, 1977.

J. Schiff, Ed. *Cathexis Reader: Transactional Analysis Treat-*

ment of Psychosis. New York: Harper & Row, 1975.

Books Dealing with Children

D. E. Babock and T. D. Keepers. *Raising Kids OK.* New York: Grove Press, 1976.

K. Ernst. *Games Students Play.* San Francisco, Cal.: Transactional Analysis.

M. James. *What Do You Do with Them Now That You've Got Them.* Menlo Park: Addison-Wesley, 1974.

P. Leven. *Becoming The Way We Are.* San Francisco, Cal.: Transactional Analysis.

6

Haim Ginott's Approach to Discipline

Arthur Orgel, Ph.D.

Any good dictionary will provide at least seven or eight distinguishable meanings for the English word *discipline*. These range from "training that is expected to produce a specified character or pattern of behavior" to "a state of order based upon submission to rules and authority" to "a systematic method to obtain obedience: as in military discipline," and so on (American Heritage, 1969). For nonlinguists, the word has an even greater variety of meanings. For some parents, discipline means rapid punishment following misbehavior; for others, it means the accutron-precision of the waking-eating-studying-playing-sleeping schedule. For some teachers, it means five hours of classroom time, where total silence is punctuated only by the issuance of commands; for others, it means five hours of "creative expression," even if the context is one of chaos, confusion, and crises. For some politicians, discipline means that the leader has absolute power to punish his enemies; for others, it refers to the willingness of party members to donate large amounts of money at regular intervals.

This welter of different meanings, of course, means

that one who would address himself to the topic of discipline must first try to define the term. For me, the most meaningful definition of discipline evolves from its cognate — *disciple*. A disciple is a person who subscribes to the teachings of another and assists in spreading them. Discipline, therefore, is the educating of disciples. It involves both a process and a purpose. The process is one of teaching, and, like all teaching, its effectiveness depends in large part on teaching skills — the careful application of sound principles of learning. The purpose of discipline is to produce a future teacher — that is, one who actively subscribes to, affirms, and applies what he has learned.

But neither the process nor the purpose of discipline can be considered by itself. Efficient teaching methodology has been used to produce monsters who run concentration camps and automatons who cultivate rice paddies; idealistic and humane parents have been known to produce tyrants who exploit others and emotional cripples who cannot give or receive love. Clearly, the purpose or goal of discipline involves a value system; and this value system in turn affects teaching methodology, for the teaching process employed is meant to produce converts rather than conscripts, citizens rather than subjects.

Surprisingly, one finds very little disagreement about the purpose of discipline and its associated value system. Whether one reads Ginott (1965), Baruch (1949), Gordon (1970), or Fraiberg (1959), there seems to be a real consensus about goals. And one can detect the same consensus in this book, which presents the view of six people of different schools and orientations. All are agreed that children should grow up to personify the democratic ideal — that they should be free but properly mindful of the rights of others, autonomous but unselfish, creative but not destructive, empathic but not self-abasing. In short, all people want their children to become civilized human beings, capable of experiencing the full richness and joy of life, while at the same time contributing to and enhancing the quality of our society and of human life in general.

Unfortunately, agreement about goals is not matched by much agreement about means. Parents and teachers are literally deluged with conflicting advice about how to teach civilized behavior. There are some experts who advocate superpermissiveness as the essential ingredient for proper development and some who advocate strict schedules, rigid rules, and frequent punishment; there are some who would use tokens and trinkets to increase the frequency of responses that the adult values and some who would have the child and adult reason together to achieve a consensus about standards of behavior; there are some who would extinguish misbehavior by withholding affection and attention; and there are some who believe that the withdrawal of emotional support results in serious psychological damage.

This confusion about method arises because the teaching-learning process is simply not fully understood at this point in our scientific development: we do not really know enough about the processes involved in learning academic and motor skills, much less about the best and most efficient ways to teach values, attitudes, and beliefs. Methodology, therefore, is often derived from theories of learning and personality. And gaps in knowledge, especially knowledge about discipline, are filled in by theoreticians who are sometimes too ready to translate what they think they know into programs of implementation. For those engaged on the front lines of interaction with children—parents, teachers, pediatricians, and even psychiatrists and psychologists—the faddish waxing and waning of theories has resulted in increasing confusion, insecurity, and vacillation.

In fact, it is the modern adult's qualities of uncertainty and lack of confidence that stimulated Ginott to develop his tactical and strategic approach to child rearing (1972). In doing so, he borrowed freely from other people — from Rogers and Axline, from Slavson and Baruch, from Anna Freud and Albert Bandura. His goal was not to be "all things to all men" but rather to extract from each approach those aspects that were most sensible and demonstrable, and least likely to jeopardize the ultimate goal of discipline. Ginott tried to weave these borrowings and his own vast experience with troubled families into a practical guide for parents and teachers. As a practicing clinician and educator, moreover, he tended to emphasize technique rather than theory. In fact, he was singularly unenamored of theoretical formulations that are divorced from tactics or that do not lend themselves to clear-cut procedures for dealing with children.

If Ginott were alive today, I am sure that he would present his approach, not as the final word about the problem of discipline, but rather as a tentative, hopefully safe, and practical guide, open to the changes and modifications that should come with increased scientific knowledge. I think that he would particularly welcome the format of this book, with its emphasis on a comparative scrutiny of approaches to discipline, because for him it would provide an opportunity and a challenge to rethink, defend, and perhaps even modify his position.

As a student, colleague, and friend of Ginott, it is my purpose, in the remainder of this chapter, to present the essential outlines of his approach to the problem of discipline. I have tried to retain the practical and technique-oriented quality of Ginott's thinking, while at the same time providing a more elaborate theoretical rationale for the material, an addition which Ginott himself might find somewhat amusing. In any event, I take full responsibility for the inevitable errors of omission and commission that befall an interpreter. And I particularly apologize for any distortions that may result from my own predilections for theoretical rationalization.

THE GINOTTIAN PERSPECTIVE

Discipline As an Interpersonal Process

Ginott's approach to discipline grew out of long years of experience as a child psychotherapist, followed by long years of work devoted almost exclusively to parent and teacher counseling and education. This background of dual experience — one from the vantage point of the child and one from the adult — lends a particular richness to his approach. Ginott emphasized the interpersonal nature of the disciplinary process; for him, discipline involves a "dynamic duo," consisting of a teacher as well as a learner. Thus, he believed that we must be as concerned with the condition of the adult as we are with the problems of the child; we must consider the reinforcements that shape the teaching and communicating skills of the disciplinarian as much as we consider the types of experiences that are most effective in teaching children; and, above all, we must be as aware of the rights and safety of the adult as we are of the needs and wishes of the child.

Discipline As Skill: A Nontraditional View

Ginott's view of the disciplinarian as a teacher represents something of a divergence from traditional approaches, a divergence which affects the manner in which he directs himself to the adult member of the "dynamic duo." Traditional psychodynamic theory tended to focus attention on the motivational and personality sources of behavior; when behavior was ineffective, it was almost always seen as a reflection of personal problems. Thus, more often than not, poor parenting was interpreted as an indication of maladjustment in the parent, and poor teaching as a reflection of personality problems in the teacher. While he would not deny that emotional problems can be the source of ineffective parenting or teaching, Ginott insisted that, *until proven otherwise*, ignorance rather than psychopathology should be the starting point.

For example, adults are often ignorant of important developmental differences between themselves and children, differences which markedly affect the intent and style of a child's conversation. Depending on their level, children have more primitive "mental operations" than adults (Ginsburg and Opper, 1969); they use language differently; and they attempt to find out about people and things in an indirect and often puzzling manner (Ginott, 1965). The uninformed adult, on the other hand, often tries to relate to children as though they were mini-adults; he answers the wrong questions, misperceives the child's intentions, and engages in convoluted, carefully reasoned, but futile discussions designed to justify his own authority or to enlist the child's intellectual and emotional agreement as well as compliance. This is particularly evident among many well-educated, well-intentioned, and "liberated" adults, who tend to respond to the content rather than the purpose of children's questions, thereby insuring that the outcome of a disciplinary interaction will be to increase feelings of frustration, confusion, and incompetence.

As an illustration, consider the following exchange between mother and child:

Mother: Johnny, go to bed now.

Johnny: Why?

M: Because it's eight o'clock.

J: So what?

M: You've been running around all day, and you're tired.

J: I'm not tired; so why do I have to go to bed?

M: Because everyone needs a lot of sleep.

J: Then why don't you go to bed, too?

M: (Losing patience) I'm older, and older people don't need as much sleep.

J: Who said so?

M: (Angry) Doctors say so, smarty! And doctors know best!

J: I don't agree.

M: Listen! I'm tired of arguing with you. Do as you're told!

J: How come Jenny gets to stay up?

M: Because Jenny is old...that's all; I've had it! You stop your fresh talk and get upstairs; and tomorrow there will be no TV!

J: You're mean, and I hate you! (He runs upstairs, slams the door, and cries himself to sleep.)

For the mother in this example, the rest of the evening is ruined. She feels angry with her child and angry with herself; but above all, she feels guilty and impotent, because, once again, her efforts to be reasonable have resulted in emotional chaos. Is her ineffectiveness an indication that she is rejecting, hateful, or sick? Or is she simply ignorant of the fact that children often ask questions, not because they want answers but rather because they are expressing a feeling or testing the firmness and dependability of adult resolve or simply exacting a price for compliance. Had mother directed her responses to this hidden agenda rather than to the content of the child's cross-examination, the scenario and its aftermath could have been different:

Mother: Eight o'clock; time for bed.

Johnny: Why?
    M: (Smiling) You tell me.
    J: Cause it's your awful rule!
    M: Right! And you hate that rule.
    J: You said it!
    M: You wish you could change it to nine o'clock.
    J: Ten!
    M: Eleven!
    J: Later, even.
    M: You wish you could stay up and watch TV all night!
    J: (Laughing) Well, even I could get tired by midnight. (He starts upstairs)
    M: I'll be right up to tuck you in.

Thus, Ginott would refocus our attention on the skills rather than the personality of the disciplinarian. This attitude evolved from Ginott's many years of work with parents, which forced him, as it has others, to recognize that the sick parent is in the minority, even among a population of referred clinic children. Ginott felt that the majority of modern parents are not rejecting, neglecting, indifferent, cruel, or selfish. Instead he believed that most troubled parents have a too-limited repertoire of skills for communicating with and guiding children. For Ginott, people who are having difficulty with children should be described as ignorant rather than mean, unskilled rather than vicious, and clumsy rather than warped. This highlights an essential optimism that permeates the Ginottian approach — the belief that the majority of people who deal with children are quite capable of improving their skills, of acquiring new and more effective methods for teaching, guiding, and communicating with children.

Discipline and the Learning Process:
The Role of Modeling

To understand the methodology that Ginott advocated for dealing with children, we must consider his view of the manner in which children learn and the conditions under which such learning is maximized. Like the modern behaviorists, whom he greatly admired, Ginott believed that children learn to cope in two important ways: by example or modeling (Bandura, 1971; Rimm and Masters, 1974), and by repeated trials that lead to success or mastery (Moskowitz and Orgel, 1969). Of the two, modeling is undoubtedly the more powerful, albeit less understood (Feshback, 1970), process. Modeling — the process of learning by example — is more a molar than a molecular concept. It usually refers to the aura of the adult model more than his behavior in any singular event — to his enduring qualities as a person rather than to his discrete actions at a given time. What precisely are the adult qualities that we would like children to model? They are the very qualities mentioned previously as the value-derived, long-range goals of the disciplinary process. They are also the qualities about which there is little disagreement. A more fruitful question, therefore, might be "under what conditions is a child most likely to model *mature* adult qualities and what methodology can the adult employ to maximize these conditions?"

THE GINOTTIAN METHOD

Step 1: The Reflection of Feeling

For Ginott, a child is most likely to emulate mature adult behavior when he perceives the adults around him as interested, sensitive, warm, understanding, and accepting. The technique or method that Ginott advocated for maximizing the likelihood that children will perceive adults with this aura, he borrowed directly from his Rogerian forebearers. Like Axline (1947) and Rogers (1951), Ginott felt that the most effective means for conveying empathy is the reflection of feelings—that is, the accepting and accurate mirroring of another person's emotional expression (Ginott, 1965, pp. 21–36). Unlike some of his more traditional colleagues, however, Ginott also felt that most well-intentioned adults are as capable of learning to use the reflective technique as are psychiatrists, psychologists, and social workers.

Ginott (1961) saw the reflection of feelings not only as a means of conveying empathy but also as a stimulus to promote self-exploration and self-acceptance. For Ginott, a child's feelings are one of the most important facets of his experience. But the child's attitudes toward these experiences—his feelings about his feelings—are determined largely by the reactions that they evoke in the adults around him. When his feelings are ignored, denied, or shamed, he learns to distrust, degrade, and distort the very essence of his experience—namely, what his senses tell him about his own reactions to people and events. When his feelings are respected and accepted, he learns that his affective experiences are safe, and he is more inclined to identify, explore, and communicate about these essential aspects of his inner life.

The reflective technique is assigned a primacy in the disciplinary process, because discipline usually involves strong feeling on the child's part. Most disciplinary situations have to do with some aspect of misbehavior, and misbehavior is almost always associated with feelings of anger, revenge, hatred, and so on. If this is so, then common sense would tell us that effective teaching and learning is most likely to occur when the subject matter is laid out for both teacher and student to see. A teaching situation in which the subject matter itself is denied, hidden, or withheld is not likely to result in much learning.

By teaching adults to use the reflective technique, we also enhance those qualities of the model that we would wish most for the child to emulate. We are building into the adult's repertoire a response for conveying interest and understanding, thereby highlighting his qualities of sensitivity, interest in, and honesty toward others. *The significance of safety.* Ginott considered the reflective technique as a means for creating the aura of emotional warmth and empathy that is most likely to increase the probability that discipline will lead to appropriate learning on the child's part and, at the same time, as a means of enhancing those properties of the disciplinarian that are closest to the democratic and humanitarian values that constitute the strategic goals of discipline. But he also recognized that reflection, like love, is not enough — that there are other important factors that drastically affect whether or not learning occurs and what is learned if it does occur. Chief among these factors is *safety* or freedom from fear. Ginott recognized that the presence of strong, aversive, emotional responses in a child — fear, guilt, pain — is likely to distort the learning progress, regardless of the good intentions and carefully drawn lesson plans of the disciplinarian. He believed that, at the very least, children are not likely to learn when they are afraid, and that, at the worst, they are likely to learn exactly what we do not want or plan for them to learn. The responses most likely to become attached to pain and fear are those that have to do with avoidance and escape rather than coping and open communication (Moskowitz and Orgel, 1969); the product of a fear-stained disciplinary dialogue is likely to be defensive rather than effective behavior, self-denying rather than self-accepting perceptions.

Why is the issue of safety so paramount in the Ginottian approach? Simply because children cannot be depended upon to express themselves in safe and civilized ways. Because they are immature and inexperienced, children do not fully distinguish between impulse and action. Their experience of their own wishes and feelings has an immediacy of expression that often spills over into inappropriate behavior — feelings of anger become a destructive temper tantrum, sibling jealousy becomes brother-punching, and a wish for attention becomes a monopolization of the dinner-table conversation. Unlike reasonable adults, who worry first and then act, children tend to act first and then worry. Their inability to delay gratification, coupled with their only partially formed concerns for the rights of others, can combine to create emotional havoc. Having gone too far, they feel intensely guilty about what they have done or said or they become terrified of what will be inflicted upon them in retribution.

It is the responsibility of the disciplinarian, therefore, to provide safety as well as empathy. By itself, the reflective technique is not adequate for this job. There are several reasons why this is so. Firstly, empathy cannot undo the irreversible qualities of destructive or antisocial acts: a hurt sister is not "unhurt" when her brother's murderous feelings are reflected; a broken vase cannot be "unbroken" by showing a child our awareness that he would like to wreck the house. When the deed is done, the evidence remains, and the emotional aftermath of guilt, fear, or shame is likely to persist.

Secondly, because it serves as a reinforcer — perhaps a very powerful social reinforcer — the use of reflection in response to actions may increase the rate of occurrence of those actions. It may actually promote the acquisition of antisocial behavior rather than the civilized behavior that constitutes the strategic goal of discipline. The aim is not that the angry child should feel his misbehavior is accepted, but only that his anger or his *wish* to misbehave is an acceptable experience.

The third and most important reason why reflection

is insufficient has to do with the adult rather than the child. As indicated earlier, Ginott was as concerned with the condition of the disciplinarian as he was with the disciplinee. His purpose was to teach new disciplinary skills to adults and to devise a methodology that would ensure that these skills could be used effectively. He recognized, therefore, that the disciplinarian must be physically and psychologically safe, if he is to be able to learn and to apply good teaching skills. Like any other human being, the disciplinarian is likely to respond to his own strong, aversive, emotional experiences with avoidant rather than coping behavior. The person who feels in danger or disgusted or degraded by a child's actions is not likely to be reinforced for efforts to communicate with the child; nor is he likely to have the attentional set that is required for teaching.

This point is illustrated in the following description of a disastrous play therapy session, conducted by a very unskilled student therapist:

> I had a seriously disturbed, borderline psychotic, nine-year-old boy assigned to me for play therapy. Never having had a child in treatment before, even I was able to see that this was a rather tough assignment. . . . Things peaked around the third or fourth session, when my patient really let loose, and for fifty full minutes, proceeded to destroy the largest and best-equipped playroom in the clinic. Drawing every ounce of knowledge and clinical expertise that I had, I stood in the center of the room mumbling inane "reflections," through gritted teeth, while the monster waged total war on the playroom. He broke furniture, he splattered the sound-proofed walls with fingerpaints, he shot darts at me, he turned over the sandbox, and he smashed every toy in the room. And in helpless perseveration, I hissed, over

and over again, "You feel very angry" and prayed . . .
that the hour would end. By the time it did end, I
was convinced that child psychotherapy was sheer
nonsense, that the child guidance movement was a
fraud perpetrated on a naive citizenry, and that Virginia Axline's book and her . . . student [Ginott] both
belonged in the garbage heap of psychology [Orgel,
1975, p. 27].

The truth of the matter is that the emotionally upset
adult cannot respond empathically to a person whose actions are upsetting him. At best, he can mouth the words
of acceptance, but without the conviction that is essential
for the empathic message to be decoded. Or worse, he is
likely to engage in his own avoidant and defensive behavior, thereby providing the child with a model that
hardly conforms to the goals described previously. Or,
still worse, he may be driven to counterattack, leveling
criticism, ridicule, threats, and invective at the source of
his distress. This last, which people who work with disturbed children see all too frequently, can only provoke
intense, emotional counterreactions in the child, resulting in the vicious cycle with which we are all familiar.
When the parent-child dialogue degenerates into accusa-
tions and counteraccusations, threats, and counterthreats,
invective and tears, we can assume that the adult is not
coming across as the mature model described at the beginning of this chapter and that the child, if he *is* learning, is worse off than if he were learning nothing at all
(Faber and Mazlish, 1974).

The safety factor — safety for the teacher and the student — demands a more complicated methodology than
reflection alone. It calls for a method that involves adult
intervention to ensure that a child's behavior conforms to
certain standards of safety, so that both members of the
"dynamic duo" are protected. But, it is a special kind of
intervention, one that is also designed to ensure that the

child will not experience and model counterproductive kinds of adult behavior, and it is one that will ensure that the adult participant is able to sustain his empathic and understanding stance.

The role of sublimation. In developing this methodology, Ginott borrowed heavily from psychoanalytic theory. For him, the goal of adult intervention is to promote sublimatory behavior in the child. Sublimation is behavior that expresses a person's feelings, wishes, and impulses, especially his "unacceptable" impulses, in safe, socially acceptable, and potentially creative forms (Freud, 1946). Like the psychoanalysts, Ginott considered sublimation as the *sine qua non* of mature behavior, because it involves self-awareness and self-acceptance that are tempered by a decent respect for the rights of others and for the reasonable demands of society. Unlike defensive behavior, which has its origins in avoidance of and distaste for one's own experiences, sublimation also carries within it the seeds of creativity. Because it is based on self-exploration and self-comfort, it also has the greatest potential for expressing the unique and individualized qualities of the person. Ginott's conceptualization of sublimation deviates somewhat from classical psychoanalytic thinking in his emphasis on sublimation as a learned skill. For him, sublimatory expression does not occur in an automatic and almost magical fashion as a function of proper development through the various psychosexual stages. Rather, it is an expressive and communicating skill, learned in the same way as other skills; namely, through modeling and practice-coupled-with-reinforcement. Hence, he sees the disciplinarian not only as a model of mature behavior, but also as a teacher of sublimatory skills, and he sees discipline not only as a means of stopping inappropriate behavior, but rather as an opportunity to rechannel unacceptable impulses into sublimatory expression. In this respect, Ginott's position is closer to that of the learning theorists than it is to psychoanalysis, for, essentially, he treats sublimation as a complex set of instrumental responses subject to shaping by a skilled teacher.

Of all adult-child interactions, it is the disciplinary vignette that is most likely to involve the impulses, wishes, and feelings that society demands not be expressed in direct actions. Disciplinary sojourns with children tend to focus mostly around aggressive, acting-out, destructive, or socially upsetting behaviors. For this very reason, the disciplinary process affords the best opportunities to teach and to demonstrate sublimation. After all, sublimation is not demanded when children are expressing sweetness-and-light feelings toward other people; it is demanded when children are enraged, jealous, defiant, and so on.

Step 2: Intervention

Ginott's technique for teaching sublimation adds two more steps to his disciplinary methodology. The first is intervention. When a child expresses his feelings in ways that endanger himself or others or in ways that are patently uncivilized, Ginott would have the adult disciplinarian actively prevent or stop the behavior in question. The technique or style of intervention, however, is extremely important, because it should, if possible, preserve the safe and empathic qualities that are so important to effective learning. Knocking a child down or twisting his arm will certainly prevent him from destroying property, but such intervention is also likely to evoke intense fear that will abort the learning process. Insults, criticisms, and personal judgments, if presented with sufficient pitch and intensity, can temporarily interrupt some manifestation of poor table manners; but they are also likely to evoke such intense anger that revenge rather than compliance becomes the only means for the child to obtain reinforcement. Long-winded sermons, parables, and explanations are not even likely to stop undesirable behavior, except occasionally, when their anesthetic qualities put children to sleep. These shop worn techniques do share two characteristics: (1) They are least likely to promote the safe and empathic features that are so important to the learning process. (2) The adult who uses them is most likely to exhibit exactly those qualities that we do not want the child to model — physical violence in response to anger, verbal abuse in response to embarrassment, and intellectualizing in response to frustration.

Indeed, there is a wealth of experimental and clinical evidence that children are extremely susceptible to modeling negative as well as positive adult behaviors. Thus, when children are exposed to aggressive or violent adult models, the frequency of their own aggressive and violent responses increases (Bandura and Walters, 1963). And it is probably no accident that research in the area of child abuse has indicated that abusive parents have themselves almost always experienced abuse as children (Steele, 1975). Thus, it seems particularly important that the disciplinary process not involve violent, antisocial, or grossly immature adult behavior.

Physical punishment. In this respect, the use of physical punishment as an intervention technique deserves special consideration. For many people, the issue is highly emotional, perhaps partly because it is often associated with strongly held moral and religious beliefs and values and partly because people are constantly bombarded with contradictory advice about whether or not to "spare the rod."[1] Within a learning context such as Ginott's, how-

[1] A very famous evangelist and TV personality recently advocated that fathers should hold the Bible in one hand and a belt in the other (Graham, 1977); but the Talmud (with which Ginott was more familiar) advises: "If you must beat a child, use a string."

ever, it is clear that physical punishment must be viewed as a self-defeating and potentially dangerous technique of intervention. (1) The threat of injury almost always evokes fear in a child, and fear tends to contaminate and distort the teaching-learning process; (2) there is a strong possibility that the child will learn to respond to other people or to his own feelings of anger in the same manner as the disciplinary model, that is, with violence, and (3) there are other, safer techniques for stopping and redirecting unacceptable behavior, techniques which are effective but which also preserve the sensitive, mature, and socialized qualities of the adult model.

The disciplinarian's feelings. All of this does not mean that the adult is obliged to react to all situations without affect; in fact, emotional reactions to disciplinary situations are often inevitable for both members of the disciplinary dyad. When a child behaves in antisocial, destructive, or obnoxious ways, it is quite normal and natural for the adult to feel angry, disappointed, or even disgusted. His behavior, therefore, should not involve a cover-up or denial of his true feelings, for deceit is hardly a desired attribute of the adult model. Rather, the adult should express his feelings in exactly the manner and form that he would like the child to learn to adopt — in symbols (words) that describe the distressing events and the feelings that these events have generated in the adult (Faber and Mazlish, 1974; Gordon, 1970). The issue here is the form and focus of the adult's responses, not whether he is having an affective experience.

Adults are particularly likely to become angry and disturbed when discipline is called for after the fact — when a sibling has already been clobbered, when the match has already been lit, or when the cat has already been dumped in the swimming pool. All too often, however, adults respond to such situations with either a denial, through gritted teeth, of their true feelings or with verbal attacks and harsh labels that are directed toward the child's person — a response that is undoubtedly related to the adult's own modeling experiences. This kind of emotional expression can be as harmful to the child and as destructive to the learning process as physical brutality. It evokes intense emotional counterreactions in the child; it destroys the empathic aura that should be preserved; it presents an inappropriate adult model; and it inevitably results in increased feelings of frustration, guilt, and incompetence in the adult himself.

Following is an example of a harmful (but familiar) style of adult expression: Mother and father have been out to dinner. They come home to find the living room in chaos. Dirty glasses decorate the furniture, a pile of records has toppled over in the middle of the floor, comic books are strewn here and there, while Johnny, age eight, watches TV, oblivious to the disorder.

Father: You are the biggest slob I have ever known. Just who do you think you are that you can treat this living room like a pig sty? Is it your opinion, mister big shot, that your mother is a maid in this house? Your laziness could get you a Nobel Prize, if they gave Nobel Prizes to pigs. Now get off your duff and clean up this mess, and don't you ever serve food to your friends in this room again!

If father is big enough and threatening enough, Johnny will undoubtedly clean up the living room; but what has he learned? Probably several things: (1) his father considers him an animal; (2) his father uses his well-educated tongue to bully other people and to make them feel like dirt; (3) grown-ups express their anger by attacking the worth of other people; (4) if ever one had an irresisti-

ble urge to punish father, the way to do it would be to
mess up the living room.

An alternative scenario:

Father: This room is a disaster-area. When I see a
mess like this — dirty glasses that should be
in the dishwasher, comic books that should
be on the shelf, and records that should be
put away — it makes me feel so angry that I
can hardly keep from yelling. This scene is
getting me madder and madder as I keep
looking at it. It's clear that a broom and
some elbow-grease are called for right
away, if I'm going to calm down. This has
to be rectified!

Johnny: Okay — I'll clean it up right away so don't
blow your top. But what does rectified
mean?

Father: Right now I'm too angry to explain words.
But there's a dictionary on the end table.

Johnny cleans the room, then looks up the word. What
has Johnny learned? Among other things, he has learned
that adult anger can be explored and expressed without
psychological murder; that his own actions or lack of action can affect the way other, important people feel; that
the appropriate vehicle for expressing anger is words;
and that his own coping efforts can serve to undo emotional distress. An added filigree is that he has learned a
new word, and to his joy, the word clearly implies that
emotional crises can be "set right."

The technique of intervention. The Ginottian method of
intervention consists of a simple, direct, and clear-cut
statement about the unacceptability of the child's behavior. Ginott advocated that this statement be made in the
passive voice, to ensure that the child's attention will be
focused on his own actions, which is where we want his

attention to be, rather than on some irrelevant aspect of the situation. The passive voice also ensures that the disciplinarian himself will be most likely to focus his negative judgment on behavior and least likely to let it spill over into an evaluation of or attack upon the child's person. Ginott's concern is that the intervention procedure not jeopardize the empathic aura so important to the teaching process. An additional reason for this rather backhanded grammatical construction is that it is less likely to evoke anger, loss of face, or a contest of wills than a person-directed command. Thus, "The walls are not for writing on" is more effective than "Stop writing on the walls!"; and "Hitting is not allowed" is preferable to "You stop hitting your brother!"

Interestingly, this aspect of the Ginottian technique has evoked much ridicule and criticism. Many people object to the use of the passive voice, because it sounds artificial or even "unnatural" to them. Indeed, it is a *deliberately* artificial technique, almost a contrivance, designed to ensure that the adult's interventions will be less likely to interfere with learning and designed to ensure that the style of intervention will be clearly distinguishable, both for the adult and for the child, from other kinds of intervention that have such negative effects upon learning. Above all, Ginott wanted a technique that would make it easiest for the adult to maintain a very important and fundamental distinction — that it is appropriate and desirable to prevent or stop certain types of behavior, but that it is not appropriate and never desirable for the adult to stop or prevent the child's experience of his own feelings. When we teach adults to focus their attention on activities — to actually start their intervention-sentences with the act that they disapprove or the object of that act — we minimize the possibility that they will direct their judgments to the child's person, his motivation, or his feelings.

In fact, Ginott believed that an adult should direct all of his judgments — positive or negative — to behavior rather than personality, in order to minimize the occurence of irrelevant emotional responses that interfere with learning. Thus, the use of praise as a reward for desirable behavior is most likely to be effective if it is directed to behavior. When directed to the behaving person, praise can evoke embarrassment, guilt, or even anger, and these evoked responses can generate undesirable consequences, a fact which is very disconcerting to the well-intentioned but uninformed parent.

All day long Susan's mother kept telling her to rake the yard. Under threat of severe punishment, Susan finally did the job, but with each stroke of the rake, she fantasized that she was scratching her "mean" mother rather than the leaf-strewn lawn. When the mother appeared and said, "Oh Susan, you are such a good girl to do the raking; you are Mother's little helper!", Susan burst into tears and ran into the house. "My God, now what have I done wrong?" thought the mother.

What the mother did wrong was to make Susan feel guilty for having entertained such hateful feelings. How much better if she had steered clear of evaluating Susan's personality and motivation and said instead. "What a beautiful job — the yard is spotless and a joy to see. I can tell that it took a lot of hard work!"

Permissiveness redefined. The second step in Ginott's disciplinary method — intervention — is in some ways the most difficult to teach. It is in this area that one encounters the greatest amount of confusion and misconception on the part of well-intentioned, modern adults. This confusion revolves primarily around the issue of permissiveness; on the surface, there seems to be a real contradiction between active intervention and the concepts of acceptance and permissiveness. How can we be accepting and yet demand conformity at the same time? In this re-spect, Ginott felt that child experts had done a real dis-service by convincing people that permissiveness, of it-self, is essential for the proper emotional development of children and by failing to define or operationalize the term so that it can translate into a sensible and useful method rather than an esoteric, impractical, and guilt-producing belief.

The effective teaching of an intervention skill, there-fore, is often dependent upon a prior or prerequisite learn-ing that has more to do with concepts than with method-ology *per se*. Ginott found that he had to change people's misconceptions about the meaning of permissiveness be-fore he could teach the comfortable use of a technique of intervention. For this purpose, he found it useful to make a clear differentiation between two aspects of children's behavior: feelings and actions. Once this differentiation is fully understood, it is possible to discriminate between appropriate and inappropriate, helpful and harmful, per-missiveness. For Ginott, unconditional permissiveness is appropriate and useful only when it applies to a child's feelings. When directed toward behavior, however, per-missiveness must be conditional: that is, it should apply only to behavior that conforms to reasonable standards of social acceptability. I am often amazed by the relief that occurs when parents, student-therapists, and teach-ers first discover that they are not obligated to be accept-ing of and permissive about every aspect of a child's be-havior.

The significance of symbolic expression. The concept of permissiveness is further clarified and operationalized if we can formulate a general principle that will help adults to distinguish between socially acceptable and socially unacceptable behavior. This distinction is not simply a matter of whim or of individual value systems (although value systems must be recognized and respected in the teaching of disciplinary skills). For Ginott, socially acceptable behavior has certain clear-cut and identifiable properties. It is behavior which occurs in symbolic rather than direct form. Thus, feelings expressed in words, pictures, stories, or play are always accepted, because they are being communicated in a manner which is safe. Unsocial feelings expressed in direct action are not accepted, because they are being communicated in ways that violate the safety standards required for good teaching or in ways that violate the basic tenets of civilized conduct.

Aside from safety, symbolic expression has a number of other advantages. Firstly, it permits the adult to enhance and sustain his empathic stance, because symbols are less likely than acts to provoke contaminating emotional responses in the disciplinarian. A verbal description of hateful feelings toward a sibling is much more likely to evoke objective attention and understanding than poking, pushing, or pummeling; an ugly picture of a mean daddy is much easier to accept than the feelings associated with a painful kick in the shins. Secondly, symbolic expression allows for more precise communication than direct expression. The intensity of hatred expressed in a smack can be judged only on the basis of the intensity of the smack—the nuances of hatred, qualitative and quantitative, can be explored much more richly in a story or in puppet play. A third advantage of symbolic expression is that symbols are much more reversible than acts. Words can be altered easily to reflect changes in feeling-tone; bloody noses, broken arms, and smashed dinnerware are not so easy to undo. This last is especially important because of the crucial role of ambivalence in the emotional life of human beings (Moskowitz and Orgel, 1969). More often than not, our feelings trouble us because they are complex rather than simple, because we hate at the same time that we love, because we are afraid at the same time that we are angry. Symbolic expression allows plenty of elbow room for the exploration of ambivalence. An angry word can be modified, taken back, subtracted from, or added to; a drawing can be erased, embellished, or redrawn, if necessary.

Mike, age five, became enraged at his therapist and wanted to attack.

Therapist: I'm not for hitting; but you can use this [small doll] to stand for me and show me how angry you are.

Mike: Okay (Takes the doll to the sandbox, where there is a huge puddle of water). This is you, and I'm going to drown you in the Milwaukee River.

T: That's how angry you are.

M: Yes, you're up to your knees (Giggles).

T: You want it to be a slow torture.

M: Yes, and the water is coming higher and higher.

T: You want me to suffer for making all those rules.

M: Yes, I want you to suffer — you're up to your neck.

T: Right now, you hate me so much, you'd like to even hear me scream for mercy.

M: Yes, I'd like to hear you scream: "Help me, help me; please don't drown me, Mike!" (Pause)

M: Well, okay. I'll stop, because you are really my pal.

T: Sometimes you hate me; but other times you like me.

M: Yeah. I guess I'll make an island, just for you and me. A place where we can be alone.

T: Right now you would like to go away with me for a long time — just us.

M: Yes, where nobody else could bother us. (Mimicking therapist's voice) But the rule is, we have to leave when the time is up. . . . I hate your rules!

These qualities of symbolic expression are also the qualities of subliminatory behavior (Ginott, 1961): social acceptability, accuracy of self-exploration, richness and flexibility of expression. And subliminatory behavior is exactly what we would like a child to learn as a function of disciplinary teaching, what we would like for him to substitute for the antisocial, offensive, or defensive behavior that makes discipline necessary.

Step 3: Teaching Subliminatory Skills

This leads us to a consideration of the third step in Ginott's disciplinary methodology — the active teaching of sublimation. The skilled disciplinarian follows his interventions with suggestions about alternative, symbolic modes of expression, alternatives that permit the child to continue to express his feelings in safety. Such alternatives also permit the disciplinarian to resume his empathic stance, to demonstrate again the cardinal message of the disciplinary dialogue: "Your feelings are accepted and respected; only your actions are judged."

Earlier it was said that children learn by practice as well as by example. It is in the second and third steps of Ginott's methodology that such learning is most apparent, that the disciplinarian becomes an active teacher as well as a model for emulation. The analogy here between disciplinary teaching and the teaching of instrumental skills is compelling. Like the skilled teacher, the skilled disciplinarian is discriminating in his use of reinforcements — he withholds empathy when responses are inappropriate, but dispenses it freely when appropriate behavior occurs. Like the skilled teacher, though, he does not simply wait for the child to grope his way toward appropriate responding. Rather, the adult plays an active, shaping role by intervening to minimize the occurrence of undesirable behavior and by actively guiding to maximize the occurrence of responses that can be reinforced. Initially, most adults need help and instruction in formulating attractive and appropriate, symbolic alternatives for children. This third step of the Ginottian methodology is the one that requires the most innovation and imagination on the adult's part. It also requires some knowledge of developmental issues, of the relationship between age-level and modes of communication, and of the limitations of certain types of symbolic expression for particular ages or for children with special characteristics, such as limited intelligence, physical disabilities, or what have you. Thus, one would not ask a two-year-old to tell in words his angry feelings toward his brother, but one could certainly encourage him to use a doll to stand for his brother, or one could draw a picture of brother's face for the child. One would not suggest that a six-year-old write a story about her "mean teacher," but one could suggest that she make a drawing to show how she feels. One would not ask a "cool" fifteen-year-old to express his feelings about parental rules with hand puppets, but one could certainly suggest that he write down his grievances so that mother and father will have an absolutely accurate appreciation of his feelings.

Philosophical and Other Objections

For some people, active intervention and guidance are objectionable on philosophical grounds. There are those who believe that children should be free and unrestrained, that adults are violating a basic human right when they impose their standards and values upon a child. The implication of such beliefs is that people reach the zenith of humanness — of individuality, creativity, and freedom — if they are permitted to develop without restrictions. Such approaches seem naive at least and dangerous at worst; they make for good poetry but for very poor psychology. There is a singular lack of evidence that infants arrive, from God, "trailing clouds of glory"; in fact, their behavior is often far from glorious by even very minimum standards of civilized conduct. Parent counselors, educators, and policemen have turned up no stunning evidence that children from superpermissive homes are headed toward new heights of human accomplishment and virtue.

More venial, but certainly less innane, objections have to do with questions about the workability of Ginott's methods. A frequent reaction to his methodology is the assertion that it is fine on paper but not likely to work in eyeball-to-eyeball confrontations between adults and children. Such reservations are understandable; most of us never had parents or teachers who bothered to reflect our feelings, set limits in the passive voice, and then help us to find acceptable ways of showing how much we would like to get rid of our baby sisters. Few of us have had an opportunity to model or practice such an approach, and initially, therefore, it tends to strike us like a foreign language — it sounds lovely, but it has no meaning. Interestingly, most people have more difficulty with step two than with step three; effective intervention is harder for them than subliminatory guidance. Thus parents will often say, "You don't know my child. If I told him 'The chair is not for kicking,' he would laugh in my face and kick even harder!"

Guidance and practice for the disciplinarian. The unworkability hypothesis is usually a reflection of the adult's lack of confidence, experience, and skill. When he tries a new method of intervention, he is trying a technique for which he has never been reinforced; hence, his words and bearing convey weakness rather than firmness, indecision rather than conviction, and expectancies of failure rather than self-confidence. It is as though he sees only the two ends of a continuum of adult strength — a weak rebuke, which never works, and a catastrophic, violent outburst, which is where he usually winds up anyway and for which he has intense feelings of guilt and shame. Afraid that he will lose control and do it again, the adult is too preoccupied with his own feelings of insecurity and doubt to make himself sound convincing. Children, of course, are masters at exploiting any indication of adult weakness; thus, when the adult warbles, "The coffee table is not for feet," the basis for escalation is established.

A six-foot-tall student therapist was having great difficulty in controlling two four-year-old girls in group play therapy. The children spent most of the hour shooting darts at him, in spite of all his efforts to rechannel their behavior into a less disconcerting and annoying form. In one supervisory session, he admitted, shamefacedly: "I keep telling them that I'm not for shooting; I even draw my picture for them to shoot at; I use the exact words that you use! But nothing works! One of the damned darts even stuck to my glasses in the last session, and I had to reach up and pull it off — what a put-down!"

While playing a videotape of one of the therapy sessions, it became obvious to the supervisor (but not to the trainee) that the limits were being given in a less than commanding style — the trainee stood across the room from the children (who shot at him from behind an easel); the pitch of his voice was a full octave higher than normal; and each statement could easily have been punctuated with a question mark rather than a period. Finally, in exasperation, the supervisor stopped the machine in the middle of the sentence "I am not for shooting." There, frozen on the screen, was the student, crouched low, with his hands protecting his face. The student looked at the picture in amazement and then laughed: "I have a feeling they are responding to my body language and not listening to my words!"

Between the two equally ineffective extremes, the adult often has no operants, no graded repertoire of responses that can be used to effect control. It is in this area that we can be very helpful, by teaching the disciplinarian a whole range of new responses for intervention. We can show him that strength and harshness are two entirely different things, that adults can be firm without resorting to violence or attacks on personality. Thus, the statement "Sister is not for hitting" can be followed by getting out of one's chair while repeating the rule with greater emphasis; getting out of one's chair can be followed by approaching (rather than retreating), with an even stronger statement of the rule; and approaching can even be followed by active restraint, where this is necessary. In other words, adults can be taught to use their size, their commanding presence, and their superior strength to gain control; and they can be shown that such responses are effective without having to be carried to the point where intense, interfering emotional responses are evoked in either member of the disciplinary dyad.

In teaching this methodology, we must recognize that the disciplinarian is learning, too, and that disciplining skills take practice and reinforcement before they can become firmly established. In this regard, role playing and demonstration can be as useful as didactic instruction. Videotapes of adult-child interactions, when feasible, are an extraordinarily effective teaching vehicle.

With guided practice, well-intentioned adults are quite capable of learning effective intervention techniques.

As their skill increases, moreover, they become more confident of their own ability to succeed, and the intervention aspect of discipline becomes the shortest and most minor part of the disciplinary dialogue. Ultimately, many parents even short-cut the entire process by skipping the passive-voice formulation and making positive rather than negative limiting-statements—"The paint is for the paper" rather than "The wall is not for painting." To the counselor, this is always an indication of rapid progress.

The adult's increasing self-confidence also has an important, feedback effect on his properties as a model, and this, perhaps, is the greatest payoff of all. Certainly, self-confidence and self-assurance are attributes that we would like children to experience in the adults around them, particularly when self-confidence is coupled with kindness, warmth, and nonviolence.

Step 4: Further Reflection

The fourth and final step in Ginott's methodology has to do with the child's reactions to discipline itself. Children do not delight in being disciplined. No matter how mild, objective, impersonal, and kindly our efforts, we must expect that children will resent and react to our intrusions. After all, intervention, even when it is phrased in passive poetry, constitutes an interruption of an ongoing, goal-directed, and important effort at communication. The good disciplinarian, therefore, takes time to reflect the child's displeasure with rules and rule-makers; he recognizes that the disciplinarian himself will become a focus for feelings; and he extends the same empathic courtesy to these feelings as he would to any others, provided, of course, that they are expressed in safe, symbolic form.

Thus, like a chain letter, discipline can sometimes

become intriguingly complex, leading in a sense to disciplinary dialogues within disciplinary dialogues. What starts as an intervention around issues of sibling jealousy may lead to intervention around wishes to dethrone authority. But the entire process is meaningful and important because it results in self-exploration and self-acceptance for the child and because it provides the child with a model of adult sensitivity and concern for the feelings of others. Surely the time devoted to such adult-child explorations is more rewarding — even more fun — than the pain associated with sullen silences, slammed doors, temper tantrums, and so on.

SUMMARY

The Ginottian approach to discipline, therefore, can be summarized as a four-step teaching method. (1) The adult recognizes and reflects the child's feelings and wishes; he helps the child to express and explore his experience in words. (2) When necessary, the adult intervenes to prevent or stop unacceptable behavior, but in doing so he differentiates between the child's feelings, which are always accepted, and his actions, which are only conditionally accepted. He focuses attention on the child's behavior, which is being judged, rather than on his personality, which is never judged, and he states, clearly and succinctly, the principle involved in his judgment. (3) The adult actively teaches a process of sublimation; he helps the child to find acceptable, satisfying, and potentially creative ways of self-expression and self-exploration. (4) The adult recognizes, without judgment, the child's right not to enjoy discipline.

REFERENCES

The American Heritage Dictionary (1969). Boston: Houghton Mifflin.

Axline, V. (1947), *Play Therapy*. Boston: Houghton Mifflin.

Bandura, A. (1971), Psychotherapy based upon modeling principles. In: *Handbook of Psychotherapy and Behavior Change*, ed. A. E. Bergin and S. L. Garfield. New York: Wiley.

_____ and Walters, R. H. (1963), *Social Learning and Personality Development*. New York: Holt, Rinehart & Winston.

Baruch, D. W. (1949), *New Ways in Discipline*. New York: McGraw-Hill.

Faber, A., and Mazlish, E. (1974), *Liberated Parents, Liberated Children*. New York: Grosset & Dunlap.

Feshback, S. (1970), Aggression. In: *Carmichael's Manual of Child Psychology*. Vol. 2, ed. P. H. Mussen. New York: Wiley, pp. 159–259.

Fraiberg, S. H. (1959), *The Magic Years*. New York: Scribner's.

Freud, A. (1946), *The Ego and the Mechanisms of Defense*. New York: International Universities Press.

Ginott, H. G. (1961), *Group Psychotherapy with Children*. New York: McGraw-Hill.

_____ (1965), *Between Parent and Child*. New York: Macmillan.

_____ (1972), *Teacher and Child*. New York: Macmillan.

Ginsburg, H. and Opper, S. (1969), *Piaget's Theory of Intellectual Development*. Englewood Cliffs, N.J.: Prentice-Hall.

Gordon, T. (1970), *Parent Effectiveness Training*. New York: New American Library.

Graham, B. (1977), *Crusade: "Why Homes?"* CBS Television Network, March 7.

Moskowitz, M. and Orgel, A. (1969), *General Psychology*. Boston: Houghton Mifflin.

Orgel, A. R. (1975), Haim was my teacher, too. *Florida Psychologist*, 25(4):24–29.

Rimm, D. C. and Masters, J. C. (1974), *Behavior Therapy, Techniques and Empirical Findings*. New York: Academic Press.

Rogers, C. R. (1951), *Client-Centered Therapy*. Boston: Houghton Mifflin.

Steele, B. F. (1975), *Working with Abusive Parents from a Psychiatric Standpoint.* Washington, D.C.: DHEW Publication No. (OHD)75–70.

7

Behavioral Discipline

Charles Madsen, Jr., Ph.D.
Jane Stephens, Ph.D.

• The parents of seven-year-old Jimmy find it impossible to have any kind of conversation because their son invariably interrupts them. The content of what he has to say is usually irrelevant and it seems that the major reason for his interrupting is for attention. His parents have become extremely annoyed and have begun yelling loudly at him whenever he interrupts, which is virtually every evening.

• A fifteen-year-old boy is placed in a county juvenile detention center for physically abusing his widowed mother. He has thrown her out of the house and has threatened others with a gun. The boy states that he only wants to play his guitar and be left entirely alone.

• Six-year-old Sam usually sets the breakfast table every morning for himself and his younger brother. He dresses himself reasonably well and when he comes home from school he hangs up his coat.

• Seventeen-year-old Andy is an average student in his senior year of high school. He is in two extracurricular activities and holds a part-time job after school. His father is a plumbing contractor and Andy plans to go to technical school for a year, after which he will join his father's business.

Clearly there are outward differences among the behaviors described above. Yet there are similarities in that they tend to conform to known rules and principles of learning. The behavioral approach to discipline works on the premise that all individual behavior is governed by the same basic principles. In this sense all behavior, even "psychotic" or "criminal" behavior, is usually reasonable, predictable, and understandable — that is, normal.

Behavior modification involves the application of available knowledge regarding learning and behavioral theory to promote the betterment of the human condition. The approach is based on an empirical body of literature and is ever seeking new data which will help guide and improve approaches to helping people function in a more adaptive and adjustive fashion.

Behavior modification is based primarily on the laws and principles of operant behavior and operant learning. Operant behavior is that class of behaviors which is largely under the control of contingent or consequent events. The vast majority of adult and child behavior falls in this class. Behavior modification is a therapeutic approach in which the contingencies influencing human behavior are modified in a systematic way, to the end that more adjustive and adaptive behavior is forthcoming.

The basic principle of behavior modification, that most behavior is under the control of its consequences, is known to everyone. Were this the only contribution that behavior modification had to make, there would be no behavioral school and there would hardly be a need for a chapter on behavior modification in a book on discipline. However, while the basic principles are relatively simple and commonsensical, there is more to the picture than meets the eye. Behavioral theory is actually quite complex and people often make mistakes in trying to modify the behavior of children because they are not sufficiently aware of the basic rules and principles of learning that govern behavior. For example, a young couple is advised to ignore their three-year-old who constantly puts up a fuss after being put into bed every night. The couple ignores the child for a few nights and then gives up because "He only got worse." Unfortunately, they have not been informed that when an ignoring procedure is used to extinguish an undesirable behavior, the behavior will *increase* in intensity and frequency for a period of time before it finally begins to decrease. Consider another example. An overconcerned parent promises her four-year-old a new tricycle if he will learn to tie his shoes and is disappointed when he fails. In the first place, it is likely that this person is not aware of developmental milestones, as few four-year-olds know how to tie their shoes. Additionally, while it is true that when good consequences tend to follow behavior the behavior will increase (tying shoes), the timing of the consequence is extremely important. When one is teaching a new task to an adult or working with young children, it is very important that the consequences follow the behavior or approximations of the behavior very, very closely. To a four-year-old the possibility of getting a new tricycle for tying his shoes is light-years away. Indeed, it is hard for anyone of any age to work for goals in the distant future.

We will now attempt to outline the basic principles and techniques of behavior modification as they relate to procedures used to discipline children. Before we begin, however, we would like to raise a fundamental question: Why be concerned with discipline in the first place?

As we view it, a well-disciplined child is one who

has learned to behave in socially acceptable and appropriate ways and who gets along with family, friends, and teachers. He has learned proper patterns of response to academic work, enabling him to benefit from the educational process. This child develops into an adult who contributes positively to the surrounding community and the society at large. The goal of behavioral procedures is to help the youngster acquire self-discipline — the sense of what is real in the world and the skill of modulating one's behavior in accordance with reality and with one's own goals and wishes. The child's primary occupation is that of learner; we view discipline as a teaching process in which the child learns appropriate behaviors. We must accept the responsibility of teaching a child to get along well with others, as fully as we accept the responsibility of teaching that child academic subject matter. A child's behavior is largely a result of his or her current and past learning experiences with parents, teachers, peers, and other people and things in the environment. We can leave this learning process to chance or we can take an active and crucial role in the process, helping children learn how to behave in ways that will promote their happiness and accomplishment throughout life.

Unfortunately, discipline has a harsh connotation; even the use of the word suggests to some a curtailment of liberties. However, in our view, freedom exists only within certain specified perimeters. Those children who are taught wide ranges of acceptable prosocial and productive behaviors will be those children who will have the personal adjustment and motivation necessary to take advantage of the choices and opportunities they encounter as adults. Through discipline, we can teach children how to act wisely in the future, thus increasing their true "freedom." If we neglect this responsibility, their futures will be left to chance associations and experiences.

Either way, their behavior will be determined.

In this chapter, we will outline principles and techniques of behavior modification as applied to disciplinary problems. Since there are many texts devoted to the explication of the basic learning theory underlying behavior modification (e.g., Bandura, 1969; Neuringer and Michael, 1970), we will not cover this material here. We will attempt to address issues relevant to those individuals who encounter disciplinary problems the most frequently, namely, teachers and parents.

THE IMPORTANCE OF BEHAVIORAL ANALYSIS

Behavior modification is a very powerful procedure. While it can be extremely helpful, it can, when misused, be destructive. Hence, we must be very careful in using it for disciplinary purposes. For example, should we use behavior modification to discipline a six-year-old who cries and becomes despondent when he discovers that he has come down with the chicken pox three days before Christmas? Obviously, this is not an occasion for discipline, but rather for comfort and reassurance. However, when this same child, buoyed by the extra concern shown him through the Christmas holiday, becomes increasingly selfish and nasty to his little brother by New Year's, it is time to address the issue of discipline in behavioral terms.

Behavior modification does not dwell extensively on past events in a person's life, because it is not possible to change these events; the focus is on the present and the future. Further, an emphasis on traditional psychiatric nosology and diagnosis has historically been rejected as largely ineffective. It must be kept in mind, however, that behavior modification does emphasize a thorough understanding of the child from a behavioral-environmental point of view. A child manifests the sum total of experiences of his or her life — experiences resulting in habit hierarchies and ways of viewing the world that the wise clinician will take into consideration before embarking on a behavioral change program. Further, the behavior modifier, like any good clinician, will patiently determine what behavior is to be changed and *why* it should be changed. Clearly a four-year-old who cries when he has hurt himself warrants comfort, not being ignored. However, if this same four-year-old habitually cries when faced with frustration—instead of seeking constructive alternatives—some sort of intervention, i.e., discipline, may be employed to teach new ways of responding.

SPECIFICITY

How many times have you heard a parent or teacher admonish a child to "be good," to "be careful," to "behave"? The child nods affirmatively and goes out and does what he wants to, only to get into trouble. Upon returning he is reminded angrily that he was told to "cool it" and now he will "get it." Adult and child are at this point at a low ebb in communication. Behavior modification should foster clear communication, and the key is specificity. Behaviors to be learned or changed must be specified explicitly. To describe a behavior in general terms is not sufficient. For example, what does it mean for a student to be "aggressive" with peers? It may mean that the student hits others or kicks others or perhaps that the student verbally lashes out at others. Aggressive behavior means different things to different people, and in different situations (on the football field, knocking others down is acceptable behavior). It is necessary to know which behaviors we want the child to learn, which behaviors we want to eliminate from the child's repertoire, and in which situations each of these kinds of behaviors is relevant. A child might be described as abnormal, then as aggressive, then as mean, and then as assaultive in an effort to specify the child's problem behaviors. What is really needed is the information that the child hits other children during recess.

Specificity is just as important when we are teaching children correct associations. What is honesty? To teach honesty, we must specify the behaviors that are a part of this idea, or value. Honesty may be telling the truth, returning the correct amount of change, or accurately filing income-tax returns. Honesty will mean different behaviors at different ages, too. Actual behaviors must be pinpointed to be taught efficiently.

CLASSES OF CONTINGENCIES

Should it be determined that a specified behavior needs changing, the modification will probably involve the use of behavioral contingencies. A contingency is a response to a behavior that tends to influence the chances that the behavior will again occur — for example, approval by a significant person. There are several general kinds of consequences that we may use to modify behavior. Among them are approval, withholding approval, disapproval, threat of disapproval, and ignoring. What we associate with pleasure or happiness usually constitutes approval, such as a pleasant comment or compliment, a hug, a privilege, money. Approval is, of course, a positive consequence. Sometimes, however, what we think will be a positive consequence will not be positive to the child; for example, some children do not like ice cream. If a consequence is really functioning as approval, then we should observe an increase in the behavior which precedes that consequence.

Withholding approval is used to produce the "hope" for a positive reaction when a particular behavior is improved at next occurrence. This technique actually functions to some degree as punishment because it is likely to reduce inappropriate or unacceptable behavior, but it has the advantage of leaving room for, and responsibility for, improvement with the child. For example, a child who usually does good work turns in a sloppy, incomplete paper. The teacher, who usually compliments the child on his work, says nothing, either positive or negative. This withholding of approval communicates to the youngster that he has not done well, but that if he does a good job in the future, he will regain the approval he has lost.

Disapproval is thought to be an expression of displeasure or unhappiness, such as scolding, the loss of a privilege, or a frown. What would appear to be disapproval to us may not be so to a particular child and may not function as a punisher to decrease problem behavior. Indeed, children will often work for either kind of attention, negative or positive, and are especially likely to work for negative attention if it is the only kind they are getting. Corporal punishment is also a disapproval, but should be used sparingly, if at all. If used, it should be strong enough to stop the behavior in question immediately, or else the child may misbehave again, resulting in a vicious cycle — the strength of the punishment increases as does the child's adaptability to such punishment. Vicious cycles can occur with other types of disapproval as well. Yelling can get more and more intense, for example. Disapproval may stop a behavior at the time, and thereby reward the parent or teacher for that method of discipline; however, continuing disapproval does not often reduce the overall frequency of undesirable behavior and may, in fact, increase it.

Threat of disapproval is quite simply the use of fear. An example would be, "Do not stay up late tonight or you will flunk your exam in the morning." This technique should also be used sparingly, because when it is used often it creates fear and anxiety. Children who are primarily disciplined in this manner are negatively motivated adults who work to avoid unpleasant consequences and who are often worried and afraid of what is going to happen to them.

Ignoring will often function as a disapproval of problem behavior. To ignore means not to attend, verbally or nonverbally, to the target behavior. Ignoring undesirable behavior, when paired with praising appropriate behavior, is the most powerful positive approach to discipline. However, it is not easy, because we are so accustomed to attending to bad behavior. Like catching kids at doing appropriate things, ignoring takes practice.

ACCENTUATE THE POSITIVE

The use of one or a combination of these kinds of contingencies should be governed by a general rule: utilize *positive techniques* whenever possible. Positive techniques are at least as effective as negative techniques, sometimes more so, and they promote pleasant interactions and attitudes. Children need not learn out of fear or anxiety. Children who do usually never learn to do things for intrinsic positive satisfaction. They must always be driven by external forces, even as adults. Children who are taught to work for positive consequences, like a compliment, a smile, or a special privilege, are more likely to internalize the achievement motive. Of course, children need to receive some negative feedback to teach them to discriminate between what is appropriate and what is inappropriate behavior. In situations where a child is in danger, or may hurt someone else, negative techniques may be preferable in order to stop a behavior at once. Although negative consequences are occasionally acceptable, it remains true that when the majority of interactions a child has with others are positive, the child will have a positive self-concept, will be motivated to take advantage of learning and work opportunities, and will be able to experience love and fulfillment in relationships with others.

Being positive (catching children doing the right things) is sometimes difficult as most of us are so accustomed and skilled at attending to negative behavior. Our society orients us to correct our mistakes. Good behavior is simply taken for granted, expected. We learned, incorrectly, that providing negative consequences is the only way to discipline children and keep them good and under control. Providing positive consequences for appropriate behavior, and ignoring minor deviations, can discipline children very effectively, and pleasantly. Children will learn to work to please their parents and teachers, but parents and teachers must learn and work to notice the good behaviors of their children and respond positively to them. Catching kids being good is great discipline, and being a positive person is great fun. In addition, we get what we give, and being positive has its own rewards beyond successful discipline.

Most parents and teachers are likely to share the view that home and classroom should be primarily positive in nature. Surveys were conducted by the senior author with over 13,000 teachers, and 99.6 percent of the teachers shared the goal, value, and ideal of a positive classroom. According to their expressed value, then, we would expect these teachers to be primarily positive in the classroom because of their attempts to actualize this value. We would expect them to have at least 50 percent positive interactions when observed in the classroom. However, when we specifically define approval and disapproval comments, and approval and disapproval nonverbal behaviors, and precisely measure and count these behaviors during classroom interactions, very few teachers achieve their value of being positive. Only 8 percent of over 10,000 observed teachers were more positive than negative when their classroom interactions were objectively measured.

A good way to begin being more positive is to begin to count; keep a record of how many positive comments or nonverbal expressions of approval you give for good behavior in a particular situation. Try to be more positive each day. By keeping such records, most of us find ourselves being positive more and more often.

THE DEAD MAN TEST

While it is desirable to advocate being positive, it is often difficult, especially in the disciplinary situation. Discipline usually involves eliminating undesirable or maladaptive behavior. The two major ways of extinguishing behaviors that we have discussed are ignoring and punishment. How is one positive by ignoring or punishing? It is indeed very difficult to be positive when employing this kind of contingency. However, there is a very important and positive alternative to these two methods for extinguishing behavior, and this procedure should be preceded by a test. This test we will call the Dead Man Test (Lindsley, 1972). The basic principle of the Dead Man Test is that if you are trying to get a child to do something that a dead man can do, you are likely to fail. A dead man can *"not* talk." A dead man can *"not* throw spitballs."* A dead man can *"not* torment"* his little sister. A dead man can emit no behavior. Instead of urging children *not* to do A, B or C we recommend focussing on positive alternative behaviors that are incompatible with the behavior in question. For example, we do not tell the screaming child to "not scream," rather we ask him to talk, to speak in words, to tell us what the matter is. It is very tempting to say "Stop teasing your little sister," but remember a dead man can "not tease" someone. Rather, we might say, "I want you to play with the new game that you got for your birthday." Children cannot throw spitballs when they are studying; remember, dead men cannot study.

We strongly believe that the Dead Man Test should be applied to almost all disciplinary problems. Most of us were raised in a relatively negativistic environment and we tend to communicate this to our children. How much more exciting it is to consider the positive alternatives to misbehavior. How much more fun life is for children when these positive alternatives are pointed out to them and reinforced on a regular basis. It is important to remember that children, particularly young children, are extremely mobile. The hardest thing in the world for them to do is to sit quietly. If we keep this in mind and accentuate the positive by providing them with positive alternatives to misbehavior and by reinforcing them for their appropriate behavior, we will eliminate a vast number of "disciplinary problems" and relate to our children better.

CHOICE AND SCHEDULING OF REWARDS

As we have seen, one of the main premises behind behavior modification is acceptance of the child at his or her own level. No moralistic injunctions are involved. When we teach behaviors that are already in a student's behavioral repertoire, we are usually trying to increase the frequency of the behavior. For example, Sharon knows how to raise her hand, but it may be necessary to increase the frequency of that behavior. In another instance, we may be trying to teach a behavior that the child has not yet acquired. For this, we will reinforce increases in the quality as well as the frequency of the behavior. Again, it is necessary to start according to what the child is able to do. If Billy can only pay attention to an assignment for two minutes on the average, then a first step is to praise him for attending that long until he does so consistently. Then, very gradually, the amount of time he is attending to an assignment before he receives approval for on-task behavior should be extended. This process of slowly lengthening the attention span necessary for reward should be continued until he is able to attend as the other children do. In this fashion we are shaping behavior, rewarding successive approximations to a specified goal behavior. Exactly the same approach is necessary for teaching social skills as for teaching academic material.

Sometimes it is necessary to begin with tangible rewards like food or tokens. Some children, especially emotionally disturbed children, may not be responsive to social interactions and approval. In these situations, however, the goal is to associate the social consequences with the rewarding value of the tangible rewards so that the social consequences will acquire some positive value, too. The tangible rewards are gradually decreased as the social rewards become more effective, and the children learn to respond to positive social interactions.

The following hierarchy illustrates a continuum of classes of contingencies:

Self-satisfaction — feeling good within oneself
Social attention — honors, medals, approval
Privileges and opportunities
Tokens — money, passes
Tangible material — toys, games
Consumable materials — candy, food

Like most everyone, we believe that the upper end of the continuum constitutes the better end of the contingency ladder. However, the behavioral psychologist will always start at the level of the youngster, rather than from some preconceived notion of where the youngster *ought* to be. For example, when a schizophrenic girl would only respond to money as a reinforcement for appropriate ward behavior, we started with money. With the money she also earned privileges and opportunities (for example, being allowed to go Christmas shopping). Since her ward behavior improved, she earned money appropriately and she spent it properly. The ward staff and doctors were pleased and demonstrated approval of her behavior. With enough approval she began to think better of herself and began to gain some self-satisfaction regarding her appropriate behavior. She became *self-disciplined*, which was our goal in behavior modification. We had to start at a lower level, though it was not our intention to stay there.

SCHEDULING CONTINGENCIES

Positive consequences will tend to reinforce a behavior, but how often and at what intervals should we consequate behavior? This question brings us to the matter of schedules of reinforcement. When we are teaching or increasing desirable behavior, we want to begin by providing rewards every time we observe the target behavior. It is necessary to get the child winning, experiencing the positive consequences, and associating the good behavior with the good things that are happening. When the child has learned a behavior and routinely demonstrates that behavior, then we want to begin to reinforce the child less often. For example, approval may be given every other time we observe the good behavior. The goal becomes to consequate less and less often by gradually decreasing the frequency of rewards. This strengthens the good behavior, in the sense that the child learns not to expect a reinforcement each time he or she has good behavior and learns to delay rewards for longer and longer periods of time. Good behavior will eventually become internalized, and children will begin to reward themselves for it, experiencing pride in knowing that they behave as their parents and teachers wish them to. Eventually their own standards will begin to reward them for behaving well.

The same principles apply to inappropriate behavior. Think of the gambler. Because the gambler is rewarded only some of the time, "maybe next time" becomes the motivation for gambling behavior. Receiving reinforcement on a partial, rather than a continuous, schedule strengthens the gambling behavior and makes it very resistant to extinction. We want patterns of good behavior to be resistant to extinction, but we want to be able to eliminate maladaptive behavior as quickly as possible. When trying to eliminate undesirable behavior, it is necessary to consistently ignore it or disapprove of it, or it is likely to become stronger, rather than weaker. To give in occasionally to a child's tantrum in the grocery store for a popsicle is likely to increase the strength of the tantrums and to make them harder and harder to eliminate. Consistent "negative" reactions against inappropriate behavior should eventually extinguish it.

TIMING

The question of timing is especially important when teaching younger children. With younger children, consequences need to follow the target behavior as soon as possible, or it will not be possible to establish the association between the target behavior and the intended consequence. To tell a three-year-old that Daddy is going to punish him when Daddy gets home from work is useless, and the punishment ends up becoming a negative consequence associated with Daddy or another behavior and not associated with the inappropriate behavior. As children become older, of course, they learn to wait longer and longer for rewards and punishment, and language is often used to bridge the time gap. One definition of maturity is the ability to delay gratification, and it is important to teach children to work for increasing lengths of time before being rewarded.

Timing of some sort is important when teaching new things to people of any age. To understand this, we urge the reader to introspect briefly. Consider your golf game (if you have one). Suppose you have a terrible slice that you are trying to get rid of and you go to an expensive golf pro. Would it help you more if he pointed out what you were doing wrong or right the instant you did it, or waited until after the entire round? Obviously, the moment after you made the mistake would be the better time to make the necessary corrections.

We would also emphasize the importance of adjudging timing carefully, keeping in mind the youngster's own state of progress. For example, a short attention span is a major problem for many children in school. Positive consequences for on-task behavior can be structured to teach a child to stay on-task for longer and longer periods of time. It may only take praising the child for working so hard and so well when he is able to stay on-task and then rewarding the child for gradually increasing lengths of time on-task. Initially, rewards should be immediate, and then, gradually, the length of time between the behavior and the reward can be lengthened.

USE OF BEHAVIORAL PROCEDURES
IN THE CLASSROOM

"If I had only one child to deal with at a time, behavior modification might be useful. But I have to deal with thirty children at one time." There is some validity in this statement. After all, dealing with a whole classroom is much harder than dealing with one child at a time. Fortunately, the majority of clinical and research experience with behavior modification in schools has been done in the whole classroom. The principles of specificity, matching contingencies to the response of the youngster, accentuating positive behavior, scheduling contingencies, etc., are as useful with the whole classroom as they are with the individual youngster.

For purposes of illustration, we will review some examples of the way in which behavioral principles can be used by the teacher who is dealing with the whole class. Consider the youngster who is inefficient, disorganized, and dreamy. While his intelligence is adequate, he has difficulty learning because of his poor study habits. How can a teacher who is concerned with teaching the whole class deal with this youngster? The first step would be to determine exactly what the youngster needs to do to improve his study habits. In this case he needs to learn to read and follow instructions, to increase the time he attends to his work, to complete in-class practice work, and to complete his homework. A second step would be to communicate these rules to the youngster as clearly and specifically as possible. Most teachers would assume that all of the youngsters would know that these rules hold for their classrooms. Yet there are many rules in life that we adults learn to ignore. Additionally, some youngsters need to have these rules and regulations made especially clear. It may be necessary with a youngster to repeat the rules daily. Perhaps it might help to type them on a card for the youngster to keep at his desk. Or the youngster might copy the rules himself. A next step would be to let the youngster know immediately when he has made progress toward achieving his goals. Appreciation can be expressed by a pat on the shoulder when the teacher passes by, a "smiley face" on the paper, a good mark for progress, or merely by whispering, "You're doing a good job!" The main thing is to use contingencies that *the child finds reinforcing,* not ones that the teacher thinks may be rewarding. This simple procedure combines specificity and communication with proper and timely consequation and has been found to be helpful in a large number of cases. Yet it requires very little teacher time and effort and, hence, can be used while the teacher continues her instruction of the entire class.

It is important to note that there are certain things that are not done in the above procedure. The teacher does not criticize, nag, or humiliate the youngster. Rather, she accentuates the positive. This intensive use of positive attention may not seem to have the potential to affect major change in the classroom. However, a paper by Thomas, Becker, and Armstrong (1968) provides a good example of the power of positive attention and the inefficiency of negative attention. They asked an experienced, efficient teacher to systematically vary approval and disapproval in her class of twenty-eight normal, reasonably well-behaved children. In the first aspect of the study, the teacher utilized primarily positive attention. This was a baseline phase during which attention to tasks, study behavior, and similar things were measured. At the end of the baseline period, the teacher was asked to stop using any praise and to use only contingent *disapproval* to control the children. Interestingly and predictably, the amount of disruption in the class *more than doubled.* The teacher then reverted to her normal use of disapproval and praise and the amount of disruption dropped back to its previous good level. As a test of this procedure, the cycle was repeated, again with the same results. Finally, the teacher was asked to stop all approval and triple the amount of disapproval over her usual rate. The results were remarkable. The number of disruptive behaviors skyrocketed dramatically to almost 60 percent. Finally, the teacher went back to her usual approach of using a lot of positive attention and relatively little negative attention, and the class came down to its normal level of adaptive behavior.

This study clearly illustrates the power of positive attention when used with the entire class. It is relatively easy to use this approach and it has been found time and again to be effective. Sometimes more is needed, however, to help the class settle down and get its work done. One alternative procedure is described in a paper by Barrish, Saunders, and Wolf (1969). The procedure employs the use of a "good behavior game." The twenty-four fourth graders in the target class were disruptive. Several pupils had been sent to the principal by the teacher for classroom misbehavior, and the principal was concerned about the general behavioral management problem in the class. Since this was an empirical study, the first thing that was done was to measure the existing level of behavior in the classroom. The behavior was carefully defined by the teacher and the principal and an appropriate baseline recording period was allowed. Following this, the teacher explained that the class was going to play a game every day during arithmetic period. The class was divided into teams and the teams could win prizes, such as badges or privileges, by abiding by specific rules of good behavior. The results of this approach were dramatic. During the arithmetic period the proportion of intervals in which there had been some kind of misbehavior had been about 90 percent. When the game was instituted the rate went down to about 15 percent. The game was implemented during the reading period with the same results. Interestingly, the game was set up so that both teams could win and usually they did. There were a few very difficult children who continued to misbehave and would prevent their teams from winning. To be fair to the others, these children were "benched" and placed on a program that was more individualized. It is important to note that this approach did not eliminate all misbehavior, nor was it really intended to. Rather, it greatly improved the amount of time spent studying during the arithmetic and reading periods. It was fairly easy to implement and, most importantly, it could be used with at least the majority of the youngsters in the classroom.

THE POWER OF MODELING

Psychoanalytic psychologists were among the first to observe that a very large portion of personality is acquired by copying parents and other significant adults in the youngster's life. The analysts were particularly interested in the process of internalization and utilized the term *identification* in discussing the way in which a youngster takes on the values and thoughts of the parent. Obviously, however, these values and beliefs become manifested in behavior and it is open to question whether the values and attitudes or behavior are acquired first. At any rate, psychologists in the behavioral camp—the most notable early examples are Miller and Dollard (1941)—pioneered the study of the process of acquiring new behaviors through the process of imitating a model. Following Miller and Dollard's work, there was somewhat of a lull in the investigation of modeling and imitation effects until the seminal work of two other behavioral psychologists, Bandura and Walters (1963). Bandura and Walters' intent was to provide additional understanding of the way in which personality and behavioral patterns are acquired through the process of modeling and imitation. The studies they reviewed, together with their own work, conclusively demonstrated that modeling is an extremely powerful means of modifying behavioral patterns. A particularly interesting finding was that the form that behavior takes following frustration is very strongly influenced by modeling. Hence, the frustration-aggression hypothesis advanced by Miller and Dollard, which suggested that aggression is a natural and nearly inevitable response to frustration, was brought into question. It was acknowledged that, while the organism may be frustrated, the form that this frustrated behavior takes may be strongly influenced by modeling — in other words, aggression is not the natural consequence of frustration.

This is an important finding for individuals interested in a study of discipline because many discipline problems arise when a child's behavior in response to a frustrating situation gets out of control. One of the best ways to deal with such a situation is to try to teach the youngster how to deal with frustration in a way that his behavior does not become self-destructive or destructive and irritating to other people.

As noted, Bandura and Walters were interested in studying the role that modeling and imitation plays in the acquisition of personality. In subsequent years, however, they, and others, became interested in the way in which modeling procedures could be used to modify behavior. Some investigations examined the role of modeling in psychotherapy, and in recent years there has been considerable interest in using videotape and live modeling to teach adaptive skills to persons who, despite insight, do not have the behavioral skills necessary to succeed in social or other realms.

Nearly all the research on modeling and imitation has highlighted the folly of the old saying, "Do what I say; don't do what I do." Indeed, youngsters generally do what the adult does, rather than what the adult says. Hence, the adult — be he parent, teacher, or other — has in his possession one of the most potent tools to influence the development of personality, namely his own person.

The extent to which the adult is positive or negative will strongly influence whether the youngster develops into a positively thinking or a negatively thinking person. The amount of on-task behavior and orderliness of the adult will tend to be emulated by the youngster. The ability of the adult to tolerate frustration and to develop alternative coping behaviors when faced with limitations will strongly influence the tendency of the child to do the same. Hence, when one is having discipline problems one of the first places to look is at oneself. Are we providing the best models possible for our children, or are we deceitfully telling them to abide by the straight and narrow, while we model all sorts of maladaptive, self-destructive, and inconsiderate behaviors? Consider, for example, the father who lectures his children on telling the truth and honoring the rules and regulations of society. Yet this same father buys a CB radio and "fuzz buster" (an electronic device to detect the presence of radar beams) so that he can drive on the interstate at 85 miles an hour undetected by the state police. What kind of model is this father providing to his youngsters? Will this same father be surprised when he finds that his son has been involved in breaking and entering, or his daughter is dealing in cocaine? Are they not, in actuality, chips off the old block?

IMPLEMENTATION

There are several ways to implement each of the techniques we have discussed — words, expressions, things, activities, closeness. Approval, for example, may be expressed through praise, a smile, money, a trip to the bowling alley, or a hug. A reward of a smile or a hug can be just as powerful as, or more powerful than, coins or candy bars. For any given child, it will be necessary to explore and discover which expressions of approval or disapproval are most effective. Be creative, and remember to vary consequences so that the child does not become satiated with a particular reward, or too used to a particular disapproval. For children, and for all of us, the attention of others is very, very powerful when used contingently. If we value positive interactions and relationships, then we should teach them and model them for our children.

There are *four major steps* in devising and implementing behavior modification programs. The first is to *pinpoint, or specify, the behavior of concern.* As we have seen, the behavior pinpointed must be observable and measurable. To pinpoint a behavior, it is necessary to begin with the problem situation, or teaching situation, and define our concept or idea of the situation in terms of specific behaviors. Then we can consistently apply the techniques for behavior change and assess our progress with that particular problem. In pinpointing the behavior, remember that the more you know about the circumstances under which the behavior occurs and about the specific youngster from a behavioral stance, the more successful you will be.

After pinpointing the behavior of interest, *records are kept of that behavior.* "How often does it occur" or "How long does it last" are the usual ways to record behavior. Taking data provides an objective assessment of the behavior. A record of the behavior should be kept before intervening. Records should be kept for a long enough period of time to yield a good sample and description of the behavior. Usually it is a good idea to take this "baseline" data for several days. Record-keeping means that the behavior is counted, and this must be done during the times the behavior is most likely to occur, and for a length of time each day that will accurately reflect the frequency or duration of the behavior. If Johnny has a problem staying in his seat, especially during math, then the place to begin taking data is during math period. The number of times Johnny leaves his seat

or the amount of time he is out of his seat could be re-
corded. The number of math problems solved could be
the target. It is hard to be out of your seat when doing
math problems. (And if he does all his problems maybe
he has good reason to be out of his seat.) Data should be
collected at the same time and for the same amount of
time each day. Keeping records sounds difficult, but it requires only a pencil, paper, and a few decisions about the
behavior to be counted: length, time of day, place of observation, and method of counting.

Make record-keeping as easy as possible on yourself; there is no need to be complicated. If Janie is lazy,
figure out what the problem behavior really is. If it is
leaving her clothes all over the room, then the number of
pieces of clothing at two specific times during the day
may be the basis for your record. Remember, too, to be
observant while you are taking this preintervention or
baseline data, and look for any factors that may be bearing on the problem. For example, if your four-year-old
has begun to eat her dinner with her fingers instead of her
utensils, and you begin to count the number of bites she
takes during dinner with her fingers, watch for anything
that is happening that might relate to this problem. Perhaps, for whatever reason, you have forgotten recently
to cut her food before serving it, leaving her little choice
but to eat with her fingers.

The best way to get a quick and objective look at a
particular behavior is to make a simple graph of the data.
Using equal intervals along the bottom of the graph, the
abcissa, and along the side of the graph, the ordinate,
label the abcissa with the number of observations, or
days if you are doing one observation per day, and label
the ordinate with the frequency, or duration, of the behavior being counted. Plot the data according to the
measure of behavior for each observation or day. This
provides a graphic representation of the behavior, and

with an indication of whether the behavior is increasing or decreasing. If, on the first day of the baseline, you counted ten minutes of out-of-seat behavior during math class for Johnny, on the second day twelve minutes, and on the third day fourteen minutes, you could quickly see by your graph that Johnny's out-of-seat behavior was steadily increasing during your baseline period. Data should be collected and graphed throughout a program until behavior change has occurred and the desired behavior is stable.

The next step is *to consequate, to decide upon the consequences to be used and to implement them.* We have discussed the effects of the various classes of contingencies — approval, disapproval, withholding approval, threat of disapproval, and ignoring. Keep in mind the wide range of tools — words, expressions, closeness, tangible objects, activities — that can be used to implement any of the techniques. Consequation requires careful thought and will primarily depend upon values, the techniques, the particular kinds of consequences that the child responds to, and what is available in the situation. Plan to consequate according to what you can live with, or it will be impossible for you to be consistent. Keep it simple. Attention is especially powerful with younger children, and activities and things work well with adolescents. Behavioral contracts work well with adolescents, too, wherein the expected behaviors and the payoffs for those behaviors are specified in contract form. The terms of such a contract should be clear, reasonable, and terms that both parties can live with, so that they will be kept. Be sure to plan what the consequences will be for both inappropriate and appropriate behaviors; do not forget that rewarding the behavior that you want to see more often is necessary for success. The belief that elimination of a bad behavior or symptom merely leads to replacement by another bad one can become a reality if we focus only on eliminating inappropriate behavior, without reinforcing the appropriate and desirable behavior to take its place.

After pinpointing, recording, and consequating, it is time to *evaluate the program*. The most important aspect of evaluation is to give the program time to work. One rule of thumb is that *bad behavior gets worse before it gets better*, something that should be kept in mind when you prepare to make your evaluation. If the target behavior is not increasing or decreasing as you had expected, why not? There are some major variables to check. Are you really working with a specific, measurable, and observable behavior, or is it too general to count or consequate accurately? Is the approval strong enough, or is it available in quantity elsewhere, so that the child is satiated? Is consequation consistent and is the child winning with his or her good behavior? Are you asking too much of the child? Is approval or attention being contaminated by punishment? For example, "You've earned your free time now, Katie, but it is a shame that you did not do better." Examine all of these possibilities, and whatever else you think might be relevant. Then revamp your program, try again, and watch your records to see how the program is progressing. Remember: *pinpoint, record, consequate,* and *evaluate* your programs for behavior change.

The following examples of the application of behavioral principles are taken from professional cases and scientific research journals.[1] Their purpose is to elucidate the implementation of behavioral programs, and suggest some ideas for you to incorporate into your utilization of a positive approach to discipline.

[1] Cases reproduced from Madsen and Madsen (1972) with the kind permission of Allyn and Bacon, Inc., Publisher.

Pinpoint: Bothering teacher at desk (4th grade).
Record: Students unnecessarily at teacher's desk (twenty-eight occurrences — one week).
Consequate: Teacher *ignored* all children who came to desk — made no eye contact, said nothing. Teacher recognized only those children who raised hands at seats.
Evaluate: Occurrences of students at teacher's desk steadily decreased. After two weeks, daily average between zero and one.

Pinpoint: Homework study time (11- and 13-year-olds).
Record: Average 4.5 minutes homework per child per school day, after four weeks recording according to child's records. Parent's spot checks averaged 3.8 minutes.
Consequate: Television viewing time made contingent on homework time whether or not assigned. Each minute of homework or review time redeemable for six minutes of viewing time. Children kept own time logs. Given extra monetary reward when parent's record within two minutes of child's report.
Evaluate: Homework study time increased to 32 minutes per child per day, at which time parents changed the study-viewing ratio to 3-1, with no decrease in study time.

Pinpoint: School failure (16-year-old boy).
Record: Failed all academic subjects first half of year. Parents and teachers unable to "motivate studying."
Consequate: School counselor developed system with parents' cooperation. Every teacher signed individual *daily progress report* (one small sheet) after each class. Decision of signing for appropriate social and academic behaviors based on teacher's criteria. Allowance, social engagements, car privileges, contingent on number

of signatures earned each day.

Evaluate: Better grades. C+ average attained for last six-week period of same year.

Pinpoint: Repeated crying (4-year-old boy, preschool).

Record: Eight crying periods each morning following mild frustrations. Whenever boy cried, teachers comforted him (picked up, talked softly, held on lap, etc.).

Consequate: Boy ignored unless "real grounds" for crying; given approval for self-help attempts.

Evaluate: One crying spell in 5 days after initial decrease.

Consequate II: Teachers again paid attention to crying (10 days).

Evaluate II: Crying almost reached original level during record phase.

Consequate III: Boy ignored when crying; given approval for self-help (10 days).

Evaluate III: Crying decreased to zero and low level maintained.

Pinpoint: Rowdiness (6th grade).

Record: Average of 8 disruptive behaviors during each 10-second observation.

Consequate: Students allowed play break with admonition: "I will let you play now if you promise to work afterwards." Students promised they would.

Evaluate: Ineffective study behavior (9 to 12 average for 10-second intervals).

Note: Rewards must come *after the fact*. After correct "work precedes play" contingency has been established, sequencing may then become effective (i.e., work, play, work, play, work, etc.).

Pinpoint: Crawling during school (Nursery school girl, 3.4 years).

Record: Girl spent 75 percent of time (observed 2 weeks) in off-feet position. Also avoided contacts with other children and adults.

Consequate: Nursery school teachers *ignored* girl when not standing; approached, praised, displayed interest when girl on-feet. Disapproval techniques such as anger, shame, disgust, or disappointment not used.

Evaluate: Girl stood 75 percent of time during first week. During second week, up as much as other children.

Consequate II: Contingencies reversed. Teachers approved *off*-feet behavior.

Evaluate II: First day of reversal, girl off-feet 75 percent of time; second day 81.9 percent.

Consequate III: Return to praise for standing.

Evaluate III: First hour of first day, on-feet 75.9 percent; first hour of second day, 62.7 percent; by second hour, 100 percent. *No relapses observed.*

Pinpoint: Thumb-sucking (7-year-old girl).

Record: Thumb-sucking occurred 45 percent of time that the girl watched television or read (mother's records). Dentist indicated "bite" was getting worse.

Consequate: Mother, after hearing PTA lecture on "A positive approach with record-keeping," "caught" girl every time she had thumb in mouth. If thumb removed, girl received praise and special checks on prominently displayed chart in living room. (Checks were to be traded for bicycle — picture of bicycle at end of chart.) Mother continued for 14 days.

Evaluate: Thumb-sucking *increased* to 75 percent. Mother sought professional help from behaviorally oriented counselor stating, "I tried, but bribery just doesn't work."

CONCLUSION AND CAUTION

Behavioral approaches have been found to be efficient, effective, and humane in the treatment of the problems of children and youth. Yet a word of caution is in order. While relatively simple behavioral techniques are extremely powerful, unfortunately, when applied incorrectly they can be destructive. Each individual using behavioral approaches must accept the personal responsibility for applying the techniques appropriately and in a humane manner. If in doubt, it would be advisable to consult with a psychologist or other mental health professional who is knowledgable regarding the area of behavior modification. If there is no such individual available, it is possible to seek consultation through a local chapter of the Association for Advancement of Behavior Therapy.

The methods that have been outlined here when carefully applied will enable you to guide a child's emotional growth in a manner which is rewarding to you and of long-lasting benefit to the child.

Any psychological procedure can be misused by a clumsy or malevolent person. Yet of all the interventive techniques that we have reviewed, behavior modification is the most important in terms of its potential to directly affect human behavior. Hence, misused it also has the potential for being destructive. Every individual who chooses to use behavioral approaches must take on the personal responsibility of applying these procedures in the way in which they were intended — correctly with sensitivity and with moral concern for the individual.

REFERENCES

Bandura, A. (1969), *Principles of Behavior Modification*. New York: Holt, Rinehart & Winston.

Bandura, A. (1969), *Principles of Behavior Modification*. New York: Holt, Rinehart & Winston.

Bandura, A., and Walters, R. H. (1963), *Social Learning and Personality Development*. New York: Holt, Rinehart & Winston.

Barrish, H. H., Saunders, M., and Wolf, M. M. (1969), Good behavior game: Effects of individual contingencies for group consequences on disruptive behavior in a classroom. *J. of Appl. Behav. Analy.*, 2:119–124.

Lindsley, O. R. (1972), Personal communication. University of Rochester.

Madsen, C. K., and Madsen, C. H., Jr. (1972), *Parents/Children/Discipline: A Positive Approach*. Boston: Allyn & Bacon.

Miller, N. E., and Dollard, J. (1941), *Social Learning and Imitation*. New Haven: Yale University Press.

Neuringer, C., and Michael, J. L., Eds. (1970), *Behavior Modification in Clinical Psychology*. New York: Appleton-Century-Crofts.

Thomas, D. R., Becker, W. C., and Armstrong, M. (1968), Production and elimination of disruptive classroom behavior by systematically varying teacher's behavior. *J. of Appl. Behav. Analy.*, 1:35–45.

8

Overview

Darwin Dorr, Ph.D.

Six approaches to discipline have been authoritatively reviewed. Some real differences exist among them, while many others are more a matter of emphasis than of substance. An in-depth analysis of the philosophical conflicts among these approaches will be left to textbooks on theories of personality. The major purpose here is not to determine which point of view is scientifically or clinically best. Rather, it is to bring together available knowledge relevant to the specific problem of discipline. Hence, while each approach has its limitations, the positive contributions each makes to real-life problems will be emphasized. Each reader must determine what blend of approaches will be the most clinically useful, as well as the most philosophically compatible.

To this end, after a brief review of each approach, we will examine the applicability of each to a series of real-life settings, using the vehicle of the case study.

THE THEORIES: A SUMMARY

Psychoanalysis

Dr. Cass points out that Freud spoke mainly of discipline in relation to the development of "conscience" in youngsters. In neoanalytic terms, conscience refers to an internal system that can regulate basic personal drives according to the demands of society. A major interest of psychoanalytic and neoanalytic theory is the process by which personality is shaped according to how basic needs conflict with and adjust to the limits imposed by society.

As a developmental theory, psychoanalysis emphasizes the role of early experiences, particularly with parents, in the evolution of the child's personality. As a dynamic theory, it is postulated that much early character development occurs unconsciously. Guilt is seen as an important factor in fostering the internalization of parental rules and prohibitions. The vehicle of this internalization is largely identification. Transference of attitudes and feelings about parents onto others influences the child's reactions to extrafamilial authority figures. Psychoanalysis also emphasizes the way fantasy influences the child's (often distorted) perceptions of real situations.

According to Cass, a psychoanalytic view of discipline stresses the importance of understanding. Through proper understanding, parents, teachers, and others who deal with children can relate to what the child is really trying to say in his behavior — a message that may be based on unconscious feelings and motivations and may be quite different from the overt behavior itself. This kind of understanding allows the disciplinarian to respond to the relevant issues in the relationship. The same kind of understanding in the disciplinarian about his *own* feelings toward the child will help to prevent discipline that is based on projection and displacement of anger.

Psychoanalysis is a developmental theory that views the capacity for understanding and emotional control as a changing, progressive process. Hence, it has much to say about the way that an adult should deal with a disci-

pline problem at various stages of a youngster's cognitive
and emotional development.

Piaget

While Piaget had very little to say about the subject
of discipline *per se*, he and the other cognitive theorists
have developed a body of knowledge that has considerable relevance to the process of child management. Dr.
Chandler starts his review of the Piagetian perspective by
reminding us of three prevailing views of children that
have endured throughout the centuries. The first assumes
that children come into the world in a state of immorality
(original sin), and it is only through very rigid external
socialization forces that this state can be controlled. The
second view is that children are born in a state of moral
neutrality. This *tabula rasa* perspective holds that
children, and the adults that they eventually become, are
solely shaped by societal factors. The third view of children is that they enter the world in a state of natural purity, but may become soiled by the sins and corruption of
society.

Rather than accepting any of these perspectives, Piagetians tend to view child development as resulting from
a long evolutionary history influenced by both biological
and social factors; in the individual, thus, certain inherent and inevitable developmental trends are influenced to
some degree by society.

Piaget and other cognitive psychologists have much
to say about moral development. Chandler reviews the
stages of moral development and discusses their implications for disciplinary strategies. He points out the importance of understanding the youngster's stage of moral development. For example, a child under the age of five is
not able to understand causal relationships and, hence,
may not understand that a punishment is related to the

disruptive acts that he committed a half-hour previous. Older children view "eye for an eye" justice as highly appropriate. Only in adolescence do youngsters come to understand that, ideally, punishment is intended to foster reparation for offenses committed. Chandler points out the dangers in disciplinary matters of the great discrepancies between the adult's and the child's levels of moral judgment. He also points out that moral thought and moral behavior are different developmental features and that behavior cannot be understood as moral or immoral unless interpreted within the social context.

Rational-Emotive Theory

Dr. Waters reviews the basic tenets of rational-emotive therapy (RET), focusing on how irrational beliefs can lead to maladaptive behavior and unhappiness, and then relates RET to children. From this point of view, the goal of child rearing is to help youngsters develop into healthy, happy, and clear-thinking adults, rather than "anxious, whining, crooked-thinking neurotics."

The aim of discipline as viewed by RET is to help children foster self-interest, self-direction, tolerance, acceptance of uncertainty, and flexibility. Much of this is acquired through establishing internal controls and self-discipline. Discipline is viewed as the use of self-controls to achieve a desired end. Dr. Waters emphasizes the distinction that Ellis makes between *penalty* and *punishment*. Penalty is defined as a type of frustration that is applied to an individual to help him learn when his behavior has gone beyond tolerable limits. Punishment is applied with anger and is retaliative. Within the RET framework, discipline differs from punishment.

Dr. Waters suggests the following questions be asked when dealing with a disciplinary issue. Regarding the child:

1. What behaviors are being exhibited?
2. What is the child's goal? (What is the child trying to accomplish by this behavior?)
3. What might the child be thinking?
4. What might the child be feeling?
5. How does the child want me to respond?

Adults may ask themselves:

1. What is my goal in this situation? What am I trying to accomplish (long-term and short-term goals)?
2. What are my feelings?
3. What are my behaviors? How am I attempting to achieve my goals (in terms of disputing irrational beliefs and taking action)?
4. How can I help this child build self-confidence in this area?

Transactional Analysis

Because many readers will be relatively unfamiliar with Transactional Analysis (TA), Drs. James and Barbara Allen first review its characteristics in some detail. Such features as structural analysis (Parent, Adult, and Child), transactional analysis (the way in which elements of the personalities interact with other persons), games, and scripts are summarized. The basic existential position advocated by TA, namely, "I'm OK, You're OK," is stressed, as is the way in which messages between persons can be rendered destructive by negotiating from an other than "OK" stance.

Although the Allens point out that there are no formal rules for TA discipline, they do raise several questions that one might ask (using the frameworks of structural analysis, existential position, script analysis, transactional and game analysis) when attempting to discipline from the transactional point of view. How is the discipline to be carried out and how does the child experience it? What messages are given to the child—that is, what injunctions and counterinjunctions? What kind of child do the parenting people need to create to meet their own script needs? The Allens stress the importance of understanding the level of the child's intellectual and emotional development in discipline.

They review discipline as it originates from four ego-states (Nurturant Parent, Critical Parent, Adult, and Child), pointing out the advantages and disadvantages of each. The Allens feel that parenting or disciplining is most effective when coming from the Adult and Nurturant Parent, although it may be necessary at certain times to negotiate from all of these stances.

The importance of scripts is emphasized. For example, the mother whose script is that she will be "inadequate" will likely handle discipline matters in an ineffectual manner, thus proving that she is inadequate. The parent who is convinced that he will raise a son who is "no good" will likely manage discipline in a way that will assure that the youngster will indeed grow up to be no good.

In practice, the transactional analyst is free to use techniques from other approaches—Ginott, RET, and behavioral therapy—but has an overall theoretical framework within which to understand and integrate them all.

Haim Ginott's Approach to Discipline

Dr. Arthur Orgel, former student, close friend, and colleague of Haim Ginott, summarizes Ginott's views on the topic of discipline. Orgel points out that Ginott was more a practical clinician than a personality theorist. Hence, his contributions are immediately useful. Orgel tells us that Ginott viewed discipline as an interpersonal process; thus, it is necessary to be as concerned with the condition of the adult as with the problems of the child.

Orgel strongly emphasizes Ginott's view that poor or good discipline is largely a matter of skill. Ineffective parenting or teaching should be considered due to ignorance, rather than psychopathology, unless proven otherwise.

A major element in the Ginottian approach is the reflection of feeling. Reflecting feeling clarifies the emotional states that exist between the adult and the child and communicates to the child that the adult is empathic and understanding. To be empathic and understanding, however, the adult first must be in control of the youngster's behavior.

The ways that one can use sublimation, the substitution of one goal for another, in dealing with disciplinary problems are reviewed. Ginott emphasized the desirability of finding alternatives to behaviors that are being prohibited.

One of Ginott's most important contributions was to redefine permissiveness. According to Ginott, adults should be permissive only with regard to feeling. A child has a right to his own feelings and a right to express them, but the parent also has a right to limit the behavior of the child. Acceptance of feeling coupled with control of behavior is the hallmark of the Ginottian approach and offers the adult a means of controlling the child's behavior and teaching without violating his psychological integrity. Orgel also reviews the importance of symbolism to children and the need to be sensitive to the symbolic nature of youngsters' behavior when trying to deal with disciplinary problems.

Behavior Modification

Drs. Charles Madsen and Jane Stephens outline the application of operant principles to the topic of discipline. Since the principles of operant behavior are relatively well understood, the authors devote only a small amount of space to explaining the ways in which operant behavior is controlled by consequences. They review the meaning of discipline as they see it. To them a well-disciplined child is a youngster who gets along well with family, friends, and teachers; is able to benefit from the educational process; and will develop into an adult who also gets along with other people, who is able to enjoy pleasant and rewarding interpersonal relationships, and contributes positively to the surrounding community. In short, the goal of discipline is to help the youngster acquire *self*-discipline.

Madsen and Stephens go on to review the importance of undertaking a precise behavioral analysis in attempting to deal with discipline problems. Classes of contingencies are reviewed—for example, praise or withholding approval. Adult attention to a youngster is seen as a particularly effective form of reinforcement. Madsen and Stephens also emphasize the need for undertaking a functional analysis of behavior, highlighting the importance of specificity with many examples of how target behavior can be pinpointed so that a youngster will be better able to respond to parent demands.

Behavioral discipline is positive discipline. Coercive, negativistic interventions are avoided. One way to be positive is to focus on alternative behaviors, an approach also advocated by Ginott. Hence, the good behavioral disciplinarian will guide a child toward behaviors that are *inconsistent* with the misbehavior and reinforce the child accordingly. The authors emphasize the role of timing and schedules of reinforcement in using behavioral approaches to discipline. They conclude their chapter with several examples of projects which implement behavioral discipline.

DISCUSSION CASES

In this section the reader will have an opportunity to compare and contrast the six approaches within the context of real-life situations. Discipline problems in the home will be presented first, discipline in the school next, and special discipline problems last.

Discipline in the Home

The case of Michael and Stephen. Michael is six and his brother, Stephen, twelve. They are the only two children of Dr. Calvin Graff and his wife, Joan. Dr. Graff is a research scientist who works in the laboratories of a large biological research center. He is a withdrawn, aloof, preoccupied individual. He can be socially gracious when the occasion demands, although he is naturally uncomfortable with people and rarely spends time talking with anybody, including his family. His workday is extremely long; he often leaves home before the children are awake, returning around ten or eleven in the evening. On many occasions he stays in his laboratory all night.

He had met his wife in a laboratory where he was a graduate student and she was a research assistant. Their shared interests in the natural sciences and their mutual social shyness made them comfortable with each other and they eventually married. Now, however, the care of the two children occupies much of Joan's time, and she has not worked in her husband's laboratory for many years. There is little communication in the marriage, although the relationship could be described as cordial.

Their children, Michael and Stephen, have been described as the scourge of the neighborhood. Screaming incessantly at each other, their voices drip with hatred. The older boy persistently tries to bully the younger boy, who works his mischief in more devious ways. Despite their differences, the two are almost inseparable. Their play is dominated by fantasies of war and killing. Their toys consist of knives, bombs, guns, spy radios, and the like. Both boys frequently brag about how strong and daring they are, although in truth they become very submissive when the older boys in the neighborhood come to their yard. They have been known to lure a little girl into the yard and then throw stones at her, and they have peppered the neighbor's house with mud. A major problem of considerable irritation to neighbors is spying and peeping into windows, crawling through the bushes, eavesdropping on conversations, etc. The children seldom smile and their stormy faces reveal their stormy personalities.

The father is rarely involved in the discipline of the children. The mother has a very difficult time dealing with the youngsters. For example, on one occasion the two boys were playing in the backyard. She called them in a very sweet voice inviting them to lunch. They called out, "What?" She repeated her invitation to lunch and they repeated, "What?" All this time they were observed to be giggling, but they kept up this little game yelling back "What?" every time she invited them to lunch. Finally, she said in an irritated voice, "All right, I'll bring it out to you." She then prepared their lunch and brought it out to the backyard on a tray.

Most of the time Joan's attempts to deal with the boys are couched in a very syrupy, sweet voice, although its artificial quality is evident. She has almost no control over the youngsters, however, and when she finally reaches the breaking point, she shrieks, screams, and breaks dishes. Because Joan finds herself becoming very depressed and frustrated about her relationship with her children, she is seeking assistance at the child division of a mental health clinic.

Sensitive clinicians of varying theoretical persuasions would probably emphasize similar factors in this case. However, for comparative purposes the unique contributions of each of our six theories will be emphasized.

A psychoanalytically oriented clinician might be concerned about the identification process, particularly in the younger child, who, being six, is very much in the oedipal phase of development. The father is rarely home during the hours that the children are awake and active. He is a very distant person and seldom interacts with his children in any positive way. Hence, there may be oedipal transition difficulties. The clinician would want to know how the twelve-year-old has passed through the oedipal phase — if he has successfully achieved this transition, if he is still puzzled about his own identity, and if he is overly attached to his mother. The clinician might wish to spend time with the younger child exploring his fantasies regarding his father and his mother and trying to understand the way in which he is dealing with the demands of the oedipal situation.

An analytically oriented professional might be concerned with the apparent lack of dependency gratification and of parental controls. The children's "lunch behavior" may reveal unsatisfied dependency needs, a likely hypothesis when one considers the mother's own background and her obvious guilt and consequent need to give in to the children's demands. If she can be helped to understand their dynamics, she may simply acknowledge this understanding to them but try to satisfy their dependency in more appropriate ways and at times when they are not threatening or hostile toward her.

The father provides very little control. The mother, because of her own personality, her lack of experience with young children, and her emotional difficulties (particularly her guilt and depression), is not in a position to provide control and enforce firm limits. The absence of well-established limits may exacerbate the youngsters' sense of insecurity. Their war play and killing fantasies may be counterphobic — overcoming their fears by acting especially tough.

The clinician with an analytic orientation might use fantasy-oriented play procedures to draw out and relate to themes of aggression and destruction, with interpretation of the reasons behind them. Greater understanding of the children's dynamics, the enforcement of firm limits, and affirmative steps to satisfy the children's affective needs may help mute their violent fantasies and the negative behavior they engender.

Chandler in his chapter on Piaget and other cognitive psychologists pointed out that there are three predominant theoretical orientations with regard to child development: the "original sin theory," the "purity theory," and the "tabula rasa theory." Anyone viewing these children would question the thesis that they came into the world trailing stardust. They have been neither abused nor neglected, at least in terms of their biological needs. Both their father and mother are rather civil and reasonable people. Yet the children have turned out to be hateful.

A Piagetian might be particularly interested in the level of the children's cognitive and moral development. While the older child could be described as hateful, he is able to moderate his behavior somewhat better than his brother. The latter, being six, is at a more primitive level of moral development. A major change in moral development occurs approximately between the ages of six and eight years. The child of age six is usually not able to understand, to empathize with another individual. When children pass into a more advanced stage of moral development, they have a greater capacity to empathize with others and, thus, to moderate their behavior through genuine understanding of how their actions may hurt the feelings or bodies of other persons.

At twelve, the older boy would be growing into the stage of formal operations, a stage of cognitive development that is more advanced than the one his brother occupies. Hence, a Piagetian might emphasize the need to approach the boys differently with regard to discussions of the meaning and consequences of their behavior. For example, mother has tried to reason with the younger child, but his level of cognitive and moral development may limit his understanding of her efforts. It might be more fruitful to provide him with direct rules on how to behave. However, the older boy might be able to respond to a more conceptual, reasoned discussion of the consequences of his behavior.

These highly "rational" parents might be especially interested in rational-emotive therapy concepts. Mother is very sensitive to her husband's preoccupation with his work and his failure to support her attempts to control their children. Her anger and resentment has led to marital friction. The RET therapist might attack her thinking in the following way: "You were first attracted to your husband because he was an intellectual and an academic scientist. His shyness, reclusiveness, and introversion matched your own, and you probably would have felt threatened by a more socially extroverted man. In short, you chose for your husband a quiet, passive, shy scientist. Now you are saying you are disappointed and depressed because he is not being more supportive as a father. What do you expect from a quiet, passive, shy scientist? It would be nice if he were more attentive to the children. But is it the end of the world that he isn't? Is your life ruined because he is not the world's greatest father? Must you tell yourself that you will be eternally disappointed and angry at him for his lack of attention to the children?"

The RET therapist might also point out that the mother is choosing to play the role of martyr, somehow hoping to be patted on the back for her suffering. An RET clinician might point out to mother that she has a right to satisfy her own desires, both with regard to her husband and the children, and that it is appropriate to firmly request more cooperation from the children. It might also be argued that she could profit from occasionally leaving the children with a babysitter to pursue some of her own interests.

A person who has a strong TA orientation might point out that these parents are almost always in their Adult or Adapted Child ego-states. While it is sometimes desirable to be in one's Adult state when disciplining a youngster, there are some potential dangers that show up in this particular case. In the first place, the mother, who has the lion's share of the responsibility for raising these children, is actually afraid to be a Parent, of either the Critical or Nurturing type. She tries to deal with the children from her Adapted Child. However, the children have received little of the nurturance or protection that the Parent state may provide. Further, because these parents are rarely in their Free Child ego-state they do not model joy, fun, or play.

It could be speculated that since the parents are rarely in the Parent, the older child feels this void. Hence, much of his time is spent in the role of Critical Parent vis-à-vis his younger brother, and perhaps even in a symbiotic relationship with his mother. Is it possible that he senses the lack of support and protection from his parents and, hence, tries to fill this role with his brother himself? These structural features might be explained to the mother. It would be pointed out that it is appropriate for a mother to be in the role of both Nurturant and Critical Parent. The TA clinician might also stress the role of play and fun in an attempt to help the mother find ways of exposing the children to the joy of the Free Child ego-state. If she is unable to do this easily, the therapist might give her suggestions on how to develop this particular aspect of her personality and supply appropriate permission and protection as she does so.

A TA therapist would probably work with the mother and father on how they have become the sort of people they are. In other words, he would help them to become aware of their injunctions (Don't be close, Don't make it, Don't be important, and Don't belong), to reassess these messages, and perhaps to make some major changes about whom they are to be.

A Ginottian therapist, such as Dr. Orgel, most assuredly would point out that the mother is dealing with these children from a position of weakness. She is at a loss as to how to control them. Indeed, they are out of control, and for this reason, it is very likely that she has consequently developed considerable resentment and even hatred toward them. A Ginottian would encourage her to negotiate from a position of strength. This mother, being an intellectual and something of an obsessive-compulsive, may often ruminate about what is the right thing to do. The Ginottian might emphasize the need to "think like one's grandparents," to be strong leaders in the family, and to make no excuses for this.

A Ginottian would recognize that this mother's parenting skills are weak. She attempts to be sugary sweet in dealing with her children. She needs the tools to be firm. A Ginottian could be very helpful here, showing the mother how she can set rules, see that the rules are carried out, focus on the behavior of the children, and also be able to express her own feelings. For example, the episode with the lunch could be handled as follows: "You're having fun teasing me. You'd like me to bring your lunch to you. But that's not how things are around here. This is lunch time. The lunch is on the table. It will be on the table for twenty minutes if you wish to eat it. If you do not eat lunch, you must not be very hungry. Hence, there will be no snacks in the afternoon. Supper will be at five-thirty." If this approach works, which is likely, Ginott would recommend that she express her pleasure at the children's coming to lunch at the proper time by saying something like: "It sure makes it a lot easier for me to plan my day when lunch can be served right at twelve and then cleaned up by twelve-thirty." A TA therapist might do something similar, but would have a theoretical reason for so doing.

Clinicians with a strong behavioral orientation would have several things to say about this situation. First, it might be noted that the mother is almost totally non-assertive with her children. Hence, when her attempts to deal with the children fail, she becomes frustrated. A behaviorist might suggest that she go through a series of assertiveness training sessions in which there is modeling and guided practice to help her be more assertive with her children (and perhaps with her husband too).

The second thing a behaviorist might point out (as would the psychoanalytically oriented clinician) is that these children have little in the way of strong adult males on which to model their behavior. Such activities as Boy

Scouts, Indian Guides, and other youth groups in which there are older, strong, benevolent males might be recommended.

It would be clear to a behaviorist that the mother's attempts to control the children are antecedent. She has not set down clear rules (discriminative stimuli), and she does not consequate the behavior effectively. Indeed, the lunch story is a perfect example of how accidentally to reinforce teasing and sassy behavior on the part of the children. The next time it is likely that the children will tease even longer because they know in the long run they will get the reinforcement they want.

To keep this from happening, the behaviorist would strongly emphasize the need to find adaptive and adjustive behaviors to reinforce. Hence, constructive activities, such as scouting and doing chores around the house, would be encouraged in the behavioral program. These behaviors would be clearly pinpointed (made explicit), so that the children knew exactly what was expected of them.

As noted above, I do not wish to imply that clinicians who abide by the six theories would handle the case in totally different ways. Any warm, sensitive, well-trained clinician would note the mother's feeling of loneliness, lack of support, and her need to achieve a degree of emotional security. A good clinician would also be careful not to overidentify with the mother. The father's puzzlement with regard to children would be recognized and accepted, and efforts made to help him feel that he is an important part of the family constellation, that he has much to offer his boys, and that he need not feel embarrassed about his lack of experience with children.

There are, of course, other approaches and orientations that would be relevant here. For example, if a significant depression were present, a psychiatrist might consider offering the mother an antidepressant to help her through the first few weeks or months of her consultation and therapy. If the children were deemed to be hyperactive, the psychiatrist might wish to consider some type of medication that would calm them, at the same time doing therapy and consultation with the family. A family therapist might wish to have several sessions with the whole family in order to work out patterns of communication and authority. An Adlerian might emphasize the role of inferiority and threat in the way that these children are attempting to gain dominance over life through their fantasies and behavior.

Discipline in the School

An over-controlled classroom. Mrs. Butler was a small, attractive woman in her middle twenties. Her third-grade classroom was in the basement of a church because there wasn't enough room in the main school for all of the classrooms. The eight-year-olds in her class of twenty children were very quiet and orderly. One rarely heard a pencil drop and the children almost never talked. When the principal would visit the church classroom he was pleased to see that all of the children had their heads down and seemed to be working diligently. What he didn't know was that Mrs. Butler was a tyrant. While she was sweet and pleasant when the principal visited class (she could see his car coming), much of the time she screamed and raged at the children for the slightest infraction. She seemed to take the slightest misbehavior as a personal affront and ruled her classroom with fear and cruelty, but her children were "well-behaved."

A clinician coming from the Freudian or neoanalytic school might wonder if Mrs. Butler manifests a sadistic personality. She was so intent on keeping absolute order in her classroom, the psychoanalytic clinician might wonder about the severity of her own upbringing and about a displacement of sadistic impulses arising from her own restricted childhood.

A Piagetian might point out that while these eight-year-olds have some degree of sophistication with regard to moral behavior, they are still very concrete and may be incapable of understanding some of her ravings about the need for strong moral character. A person coming from the RET point of view might wonder what irrational ideas drive Mrs. Butler to behave as she does. Does she believe that if there is some noise in the classroom she is a failure as a teacher? Does she feel that it will be the end of the world if she doesn't effectively teach every single one of the children in her class? She is quick to anger, and most people that are quick to anger usually hold some irrational ideas about themselves and others, including "musts," "shoulds," "must nots," and other absolutist statements. If the RET clinician had a good enough relationship with the teacher, he might be able to point out to her how she is contributing toward raising neurotic children who are incorporating the irrational ideas of their parents and teachers and growing into angry, hateful, and/ or guilt-ridden adults.

A clinician coming from the TA point of view might be interested in the messages that this teacher is receiving from the principal. What is the transaction between the two? Is she functioning as Critical Parent in order to carry out the principal's wishes? The TA clinician might also point out that the teacher stays in the Critical Parent almost all of the time and directs all of her transactions with pupils to the Child portion of the personality (particularly to certain unpleasant and unhappy Child ego-states). This gives the youngsters very little opportunity to exercise the Free Child or the budding Adult, which is unfortunate since only one small aspect of the personality is being exercised for six hours a day. The teacher herself, by working so hard to be perfect, probably sets herself up for an inner sense of failure.

A Ginottian may point out that the teacher is attacking the personality and character of the children rather than their behavior and that she needs to learn ways of expressing her anger without doing this.

A behavioral psychologist would immediately note that the expectancies this teacher holds for her pupils do not pass the "dead man test" (dead men can be quiet). She is placing much more emphasis on being at one's seat with one's eyes staring at a paper instead of on learning, doing problems, reading, practicing writing, and all the other things that third graders are supposed to be doing in order to learn. A behaviorist would also be very concerned about the use of negative control. There is very little in the way of positive reinforcement, critical comments outnumbering positive comments at least a hundred to one. A behaviorist would also point out that the teacher is modeling cruel and sadistic behavior that will likely beget cruel and sadistic behavior on the part of the children.

A poorly controlled classroom. Miss Weemis teaches ninth-grade English. She has been teaching for ten years, but her teaching is still only marginally adequate. She is distractible, disorganized, and inconsistent. Her classes are usually very noisy; the students, unruly and disruptive. Each year she becomes increasingly more hostile toward her students — yelling, screaming, throwing erasers, and having other tantrums. The students know that they can induce this state and usually snicker and laugh when they have her at their mercy. Miss Weemis has no family except her aging mother whom she supports. Since she has acquired some seniority as a teacher, thus assuring a good income, she feels it is not possible for her to change her profession. She is very depressed and is developing psychosomatic symptoms, such as stomach pains and high blood pressure.

A psychoanalytic clinician might be particularly interested in Miss Weemis's own personal adjustment and mental health. Obviously, she is perfectly "sane," but her forgetfulness, disorganization, and inconsistency might well reflect some personal turmoil that could profit from attention. The clinician might ask: Is she forgetful because she basically doesn't want to teach? Or does it reflect resentment over the need to support her mother? Has she dealt adequately with the death of her father? Did she have brothers and sisters, and where is her place psychologically in the family? Why did she choose the profession of teaching, which demands that one be orderly and conscientious, as well as nurturant and giving? Did she go into teaching to serve the wrong needs? How is she dealing with the still rather primitive sexuality of ninth-grade youngsters?

Cognitive psychologists such as Kohlberg have contributed greatly toward our understanding of adolescents. Does Miss Weemis adequately understand the psychology of the fourteen-year-old's rapidly growing body, the awareness of sexuality, the identity crisis? Indeed, is their identity confusion too close to her own, perhaps thereby arousing anxiety in her?

A rational-emotive therapist might focus on the matter of choice. Miss Weemis feels that she *cannot* leave teaching because she *has* to support her aging mother. Perhaps she is simply not cut out to be a teacher and had better move into some other area. Is she perhaps trying to satisfy someone else's demand? Has she looked at the alternatives that are available to her? Is her own personal

life impoverished? Has she reached out to meet friends
and to enrich her social life and, hence, her happiness?
Perhaps she simply is not cut out to teach ninth-grade
English, but would be very good at teaching English at
some other level. Has she been reluctant to approach the
principal about making such a transfer for fear that he
would reject her?

Like the psychoanalytically oriented clinician, the
RET psychologist might suggest that Miss Weemis consider therapy, in this case of the RET variety.

A transactional analyst would be particularly interested in Miss Weemis's personal life script. She seems to
have arranged her life around being sort of a sad sack
destined to work at a job that she doesn't like, and only
to be marginally successful at that. The TA psychologist
might also be interested in what kinds of transactions occur between Miss Weemis and her students. She is inconsistent. One way of understanding this inconsistency
would be within the transactional model. Is she sometimes Critical Parent, sometimes Adult, and sometimes
Child? Every teacher, of course, will slide back and forth
among these different ego-states from time to time, but
inappropriate variability in a teacher can lead to confusion on the part of the students. Alternatively, she may
be negotiating with the students from the position of a
defeated, inadequate Adapted Child. Certainly her tantrums and subsequent breakdowns are carried out in a
Child ego-state. The youngsters' snickering at her shows
that they clearly understand this. Is Miss Weemis's Adult
fully developed and does she have the capacity to deal
with the youngsters in her charge from this position?

The Ginottian would recognize that Miss Weemis
needs skills in limiting behavior. The book *Teacher and
Child* by Ginott might be suggested to her, and she might
be coached in methods of setting limits and asserting her

authority in a manner that does not escalate misbehavior.

A behavioral therapist might help Miss Weemis develop and establish a set of clear, reasonable, and enforceable rules for classroom behavior and establish positive consequences for compliance with these rules. The behaviorist might also stress the importance of identifying positive alternatives to misbehavior. Disorganized, unprepared teachers often have classroom control problems because their pupils do not have assignments of appropriate difficulty on which to work. Miss Weemis might be coached on ways of using positive comments to reinforce on task behaviors, and she might be supported in her attempts to ignore minor misbehaviors. Finally, a behaviorist might discuss the possibility of using programmed instructional materials and teaching machines as these technological aids might provide the students with appropriately graded work materials, which would allow her the time she needs to order and organize her thoughts.

A good classroom disciplinarian. Teachers and pupils are human and are, thus, imperfect. No teacher achieves "ideal" discipline in the classroom. However, the majority of teachers are good disciplinarians, and they manifest many of the principles advocated by each of our six points of view. Hence, we will describe a hypothetical teacher who provides a model of good discipline in the classroom.

Our teacher, whom we will call Mrs. Rodriguez, is fallible. There are days that she becomes irritable. Sometimes she is not firm enough and other times she is too firm. She makes mistakes and she is occasionally irrational. She is not equally effective with every youngster in her class and she is not equally competent in teaching the various subjects within her curriculum. However, she is always striving to improve her teaching. She enjoys teaching. She has a positive regard for most children, as well as for herself. Additionally, she manifests many important characteristics and she possesses many important skills that are emphasized by the various theories we have reviewed.

Perhaps Mrs. Rodriguez's most important characteristic, as viewed from the vantage point of psychoanalysis, is that she has a basic awareness and understanding of herself. She has not been formally psychoanalyzed; indeed, she has never been in psychotherapy. But between her own upbringing by sensitive and knowledgable parents and her studies in the fields of psychology and education, she has come to understand her own fantasies and emotions, both conscious and unconscious. Additionally, she is sensitive to the psychological needs and structures of her pupils. She understands their fantasies and their fears. She is perceptive of their transitory motivations. Because she understands each child's psychology, she is usually able to judge when to be firm and when to let up. For example, one youngster in her classroom became very sassy and obnoxious and threatened to hit her. However, because Mrs. Rodriguez had made the effort to get to know all of her children, she was aware that this boy's parents were having a serious marital problem. Hence, her image as a teacher was not threatened when the boy physically confronted her in the classroom. She backed off for a moment and got someone to watch her class for her. She asked: "I'm wondering if you are upset about something and if you'd like to tell me about it? Sometimes things happen at home and then it's hard to get along in school that day." This strong, potentially dangerous boy began to cry. He had been up all night. His parents had had a terrible fight and his father, whom he loved deeply, had left the home, possibly for good. The boy was allowed to stay in the principal's office, doing some work until the day was over. Later that week Mrs. Rodriguez told the boy that it was not right that he threw the tantrum that he did in the classroom and that he should not do this again. She had, however, opened the door for him to talk about his problems.

Mrs. Rodriguez is not a specialist in Piagetian psychology. In the course of her education she has learned about cognitive development so that she understands where her children are in terms of cognitive development. She understands their capacity to empathize with other youngsters. She knows about where they are in terms of moral development. She knows what they can understand in terms of causal relationships and she usually is able to gauge her teaching to the level of the youngsters' cognitive understanding.

Mrs. Rodriguez has learned not to be a blamer. While she often wishes that parents would become more involved with their children's education, she doesn't engage in the blame game ("Doesn't it all go back to the parents; there's nothing I can do"). She doesn't waste her time ruminating about how kids "should be" and how she "ought" to succeed as a teacher. She realizes that she is not a perfect teacher, nor a perfect person. She has accepted the personal responsibility of doing her best within the situation in which she works. She tries to distinguish between penalty and punishment in controlling her children. She is also sensitive to the irrational ideas that her children hold about themselves. For example, she understands that school is very difficult and that failure is often followed by frustration followed by defensiveness. All this makes it a primary seedbed for "discipline problems." While she tries to convince her students that failure is unpleasant but not the end of the world, she has learned to be confrontive in a somewhat humorous fashion when a child gets upset over failure. However, she is also able to communicate to the children that they have personal responsibilities: for example, they must learn the work, and it is fruitless to blame their problems on someone else.

When Mrs. Rodriguez started teaching, she had to work very hard on her feelings of adequacy. While she came from a good home, she had picked up a tinge of "I'm No Good." She has learned to accept the fact that she is "OK" and she has learned to treat her children as "OK." She has learned how easy it is to hook the Maladaptive Child in her children. Hence, she tries whenever possible to negotiate from her Adult in an effort to hook that Adult within the Child, a reasonable strategy within the instructional context. She also realizes that the Free Child is very important to the developing youngster and she makes sure to allow for enough time for her pupils to express this aspect in play periods. She realizes that when dealing with parents, she is also likely to negotiate from her Critical Parent to their Maladaptive Child. Again she attempts to shortcircuit this by transacting from her Nurturant Parent, as well as from her Adult.

Along the way Mrs. Rodriguez has found time to read Ginott's *Between Parent and Child* and *Teacher and Child*. She has learned that she has a right to her own anger and she has learned some techniques for expressing this anger in the classroom. Hence, she allows herself fuss periods in which she clearly communicates to her children what annoys her and why it annoys. She is usually able to avoid attacking a child personally, directing her ire instead at the behavior in question or the object of the behavior. She has several tough kids in her class who aren't doing very much work. She always tries to encourage their efforts when they do perform, but she has learned the hard way not to compliment them directly since this causes them to be embarrassed and lose face with their other tough comrades. She comments instead on how difficult that work was to do, what a good job the youngster has done, and how it is encouraging to her when she sees that kind of work, etc.

Most behavioral clinicians would probably feel that Mrs. Rodriguez applies behavioral principles accurately at most times. She is specific regarding the rules of classroom behavior and she is organized. She knows that, to learn, children need practice and repetition and that they need to exercise both long- and short-term memory. She understands shaping procedures — how to teach children to approximate a final product slowly — although she would probably find the term "shaping" somewhat distasteful. She tries to "catch kids at doing the right thing" whenever she can. While she can and does teach the whole class, she recognizes that every child progresses at his or her own speed and she puts in the extra time and effort to understand and gauge each youngster's seat work and homework. She tries whenever possible to address each child individually. She, together with the child, sets individual goals and makes sure that all the other children know when the particular youngster has achieved a goal.

Special Topics in Discipline

When not to discipline. Bill, a twelve-year-old boy, had a long history of maladjustment. He had been in and out of several classes for emotionally disturbed children and was known to every child guidance clinic in the many cities where he and his family had lived. Because of his father's job, it was necessary for the family to move often. Bill was considered to be a "pain" by teachers and students alike. He had no friends and could not learn very well because of problems with concentration. Bill was a likable boy in some ways, although he was hyperactive and very argumentative. Most attempts to try to reason with him were met with a long string of excuses. He was both encopretic and enuretic during the day and consequently suffered a great deal of rejection and teasing at the hands of other children. Mother was a poor housekeeper and when she became particularly sloppy, Bill's problems with odor grew worse.

During the course of family therapy, it became clear that this was an extremely disturbed family. The father was particularly hostile toward this boy and could find little good in him. He tried to manage the boy by barking out orders, which invariably led to Bill's retaliating and a subsequent ugly scene. Father actually seemed to set up situations in which there would be some kind of excuse to cuff the boy around. The other children in the family also had significant behavioral and emotional problems, but the family did not seem to recognize them. The parents did not admit to or recognize their own marital problems, which were extreme.

Finally, in a particularly stormy session, the mother broke into tears and admitted that her marriage was dead, that the entire family had problems, and that they were attempting to avoid dealing with their problems by focusing on Bill, who was the family scapegoat.

Over the next two years, the family slowly disintegrated. The children were placed with relatives, the mother and father separated and eventually divorced. Not surprisingly, many of Bill's discipline problems improved. He became more attentive at school, his encopresis and enuresis disappeared, he paid more attention to his personal hygiene, and he managed to stay out of arguments more. He continued to have adjustment problems, which were dealt with directly by the school personnel, but his problems were nowhere as severe as they had been when he was the scapegoat for the entire family's psychopathology.

This case highlights a significant aspect of the clinical management of discipline problems. Multiple factors contribute to behavior; hence, multiple factors contribute to the development of discipline problems. Effective work with children often requires an understanding of the family constellation and of the possibility of adult psychopathology. This case also reflects a question that many clinicians face: Does one deal only with the presenting problem if the family is unwilling to face the possibility that other factors may be contributing to the problem? Some clinicians are willing to do this with the hope that they will keep the family in therapy long enough for these other problems to come out and be dealt with (this was the approach used in this case). On the other hand, this strategy is time-consuming. Other clinicians are willing to take a much more confrontive approach, accepting the risk that they may drive the family away from potential help. Some clinicians would maintain that a focus on Bill's discipline problems would be totally inappropriate since his behavioral maladjustment was a function of the family's psychopathology and their practice of scapegoating him. Bill did, however, continue to have some behavioral problems after the family split up, which suggests that some immediate attention to his behavioral problems would have been reasonable. Perhaps the wisest approach would have been to approach Bill's behavioral problems directly, while at the same time working indirectly on the family pathology.

Lying. Mrs. Fairweather was very concerned that her

four-year-old Kathy was fibbing, and she was determined to keep her daughter from developing into a liar.

A Piagetian would immediately point out that a
four-year-old has no idea what a lie is. Indeed, even a
five-year-old does not know the difference between a
mistake and a lie. If a bright five-year-old is presented
with the equation $2+2=5$ and asked if this is a lie, the
youngster will say, "Yes, it is a lie." Obviously, the difference between a lie and a mistake is that a lie is intentional
and a mistake is an oversight. Since four- and even five-
year-olds are not able to understand intent, they are not
able to understand what a lie is.

The psychoanalytically oriented clinician's main interest would be in the developmental aspects of the problem behavior. Often, helping a parent to understand the
extent and normalcy of fantasy in a child of this age is
sufficient to allay her fears that the child is "abnormal"
and to help her deal instead with the behavior as fantasy.
If this is not sufficient, then the psychoanalytic or TA
clinician might explore why the mother was so adamant
about the matter of lying. Was she projecting her own
tendencies toward not telling the truth? Did she have a
relative who was a psychopathic liar and was she determined to prevent her youngster from growing up like her
"Uncle Harry"? Or was she merely a conscientious, morally oriented person who wanted to raise her children in
the proper way?

Someone with a Ginottian point of view would
probably recommend that the mother try to understand
that sometimes when a youngster "lies" it is often a statement of wish. Hence, one way to respond to "My nursery
school teacher gave us cake today" would be "That would
be nice if the nursery school teacher had given you cake.
You really wish that you had had cake today and maybe

you would like some cake now."

A Ginottian or a proponent of TA would also suggest to the mother that she avoid setting the child up to lie. For example, if a mother knows very well that a child has done something wrong, the question "Did you break such and so?" is an entrapment that complicates the issue. A Ginottian or a TA proponent would strongly recommend that the mother first make it clear that she knows what happened ("You drew a picture on the wall") then go on to deal with the problem ("Walls are not for drawing on. Now the wall is a mess and that hurts me" – "makes me angry," "makes me feel like screaming," etc.).

Mary Lee: The importance of physical factors. Mary Lee was a hyperactive two-year-old. Her parents were well-intended people who were pretty much run ragged by her activity. Her mother was pregnant and had recently had an operation on her foot, so she couldn't walk very well. The father was working three jobs to make enough money to pay the family's bills. Mary Lee was brought in for consultation because the parents needed some guidance on how to deal with her.

The Piagetians and other cognitive developmental psychologists would be helpful here because they could provide considerable information that would help the parents' understanding of what is normal for a two-year-old. The Ginottian approach would not be too helpful because it relies on oral communication, and a two-year-old is not really at the level where this is practical. Behavioral approaches, of course, can be quite helpful with a two-year-old, since there is no need for cognitive mediation of certain behavioral principles.

The following factors, however, suggest that there might be some other features that transcend the contributions that the various theories could make. The parents were discussing the problem of a bottle at bedtime and how the youngster was insistent on getting her bottle. This caused difficulties when they tried to get her settled for bed. The child was allergic to milk and, hence, her bottle consisted of eight ounces of room-temperature tea. The clinicians working on the case asked the parents how often she got this tea and it was found that she got four 8-ounce bottles of tea a day! This is 32 ounces of tea. It would be equivalent in terms of volume to about 160 ounces of tea for an adult of 130 pounds! The youngster was ingesting an enormous amount of caffeine each day. It was not surprising that she was agitated. The parents were advised to discontinue all liquids containing stimulants, including tea, coffee, and Coke. Not surprisingly, Mary Lee's hyperactivity settled down considerably.

This case is particularly instructive for nonmedical clinicians. While it is true that in a vast majority of cases the behavioral problems are a function of the psychology and behavioral factors within the home, there are some physical factors that need to be considered that can contribute to behavioral problems in youngsters.

Corporal punishment. Corporal punishment is a major controversy in psychological and educational circles, as well as in the broader public arena. It is a topic that elicits a great deal of emotion, and this emotion has largely obfuscated the problem. For example, few discussions of corporal punishment, either pro or con, demonstrate the wide range of activities that constitute corporal punishment. To ask a person if he or she is for or against corporal punishment is an overly simplified question. Corporal punishment is any punishment that uses physical means. But these means could vary from a light tap on an open hand to a light swat on the buttocks to hard, prolonged spanking to a slap in the face to shaking a child roughly to methods that use extreme force — such as, hitting the child with a doubled up fist, throwing the child across the room, using dangerous physical objects to brutalize the child, and a host of other tortures that are more common than is generally believed. All of these are corporal punishment, and yet it is foolish to speak of them as the same thing. Parents who adamantly agree that a slap on an open palm is a highly desirable corporal punishment may be adamantly against spanking of the bare buttocks. Preliminary research indicates that even those individuals who use corporal punishment to discipline children have strong feelings about how far to go.

The issue of corporal punishment has not been addressed in equal measure by all of our authors. Each theory, however, has something to say about the subject. Hence, these contributions will be reviewed using the case of Johnny as a departure point.

Johnny, a very active six-year-old boy, was described by his parents and teachers as destructive. Each week something was broken, including dishes, toys, crayons, windows, and tools that he was not supposed to play with. His parents had tried to scold him, reason with him, and threaten him; they had finally, in desperation, resorted to beating him rather severely when he broke things.

The first factor that a clinician with a strongly psychoanalytic orientation would consider is the fantasies that both the parents and the child may be experiencing prior to, during, and after the corporal punishment. Psychoanalytic oriented clinicians tend to stress the importance of understanding the symbolic nature of objects and actions. They would stress that the boy is in a psychosexual stage during which his fantasy life is likely to be laden with diffuse pregenital sexual thoughts and feelings. An analytic clinician may point out that some children actually invite corporal punishment as it elicits in them a primitive sexual pleasure.

A psychoanalytic clinician may also cite the danger of displaced adult anger. Corporal punishment often occurs when the parent or teacher is extremely frustrated, venting his or her anger on some object that is not capable of retaliation. The adult's anger may often be unrelated or disproportionate in relation to the child's transgression. In the case of child abuse the abusing adult may unconsciously seek nurturance (mothering) from the child and, when this does not happen, physically attack the child in an infantile rage.

Psychoanalytic writers have stressed the importance of frustration in child development. While analytic writers believe that some frustration is a desirable and/or even necessary prerequisite for emotional development, they are particularly sensitive to the damaging results of overly frustrating a child. An example from my clinical experience will illustrate this. A twelve-year-old boy in the sixth grade was referred to me for consultation regarding his encopresis. He usually held his bowel movements for days until he soiled himself, often at school. His encopresis had been a problem for many years. He was unpopular with other children, and his teachers, though patient, became irritated and disgusted thus increasing his sense of rejection and isolation. His human figure drawing was well executed except for the crotch area which had been drawn and erased so many times there was a hole in the paper.

In interview, the boy's mother told me the following story about her son's toilet training. When the boy was about thirteen months old, she was carrying another child and went into labor. Her mother — the boy's grandmother — came to take care of him while she went to the hospital. As the mother was leaving for the hospital, grandmother announced that she would toilet train the boy while mother was in the hospital so she would not have to be concerned about this when she returned home with a new baby. Grandmother used severe corporal punishment in training the child and he was indeed toilet trained when mother returned from the hospital. However, years later he was still having difficulties with encopresis. It is not unreasonable to suggest that the boy's encopresis may have been related to the severity of his early toilet training.

Piagetians and other cognitive psychologists would point out that a child at the age of six is at a primitive level of moral development. Whatever the intentions of the parent or teachers, a spanking is likely to be seen as revengeful retaliation. It is difficult for the six-year-old to understand why he is being attacked by the parent, particularly if there is a substantial time lapse between the transgression and the spanking. Piagetians might also point out that because the six-year-old is at a fairly primitive level of moral development, he or she is not able to empathize with others very well. Hence, a six-year-old may not understand the hurt that mother experiences when, say, a precious tea cup belonging to her great-grandmother is smashed and may be bewildered by the subsequent severe spanking. Finally, Piagetians might argue that corporal punishment can arrest moral development because one is taught to avoid wrongdoing out of fear of punishment instead of our of a recognition that the wrongdoing may harm self or others.

The RET clinician may stress that spanking Johnny is not a rational act. Is it not irrational for a fully grown, strong, healthy adult to use such a procedure to try to modify the behavior of a little child? The RET therapist might question what inappropriate emotions the parents were feeling and what irrational thoughts they were thinking when using corporal punishment. For example, is mother feeling anger because she's thinking, "If he breaks one more thing I will *not* be able to stand it.... He *must* behave.... He *should* behave," etc.? Or perhaps father is angry with his wife's inability to control Johnny's destructive behavior because he is thinking to himself, "My wife *should* be able to control him and if she can't I will become extremely angry." Finally, the RET clinician would likely stress the difference between penalty and punishment, citing spanking as a punishment.

The transactional analyst might observe that when a parent or teacher spanks a child he or she may be in a Child ego-state. When in the Child state, the parent is likely to be as irrational and demanding of the child as the child is of the parent. Child-Child communications in discipline are extremely dangerous because of the possibility of physical harm which this puts on him. By using corporal punishment, the parent is telling the youngster that it is all right to strike out at other perons when in the Child state. Finally, corporal punishment gives the child many negative strokes and deprives him of an opportunity for creative problem solving.

Ginottian clinicians might observe that the disciplinarian has been unskillful in applying the positive alternative procedures in modifying the child's behavior. They would also be concerned with the psychodynamic features of corporal punishment, including some of its implications. Finally, the Ginottian would stress that corporal punishment usually stimulates resentment in the youngster and a desire to retaliate which, in turn, may foster more misbehavior rather than less.

Behavioral psychologists have several things to say about corporal punishment. First, they might cite Bandura's (1960) research demonstrating the modeling effects of corporal punishment. Bandura found that while children who receive corporal punishment and discipline were less agressive at home, they were more aggressive in the community, presumably because they have been exposed to an aggressive parental model. Behaviorists would also cite research indicating that corporal punishment tends to suppress all behavior, not just the behavior in question. This leads to a third problem: corporal punishment does not encourage the development of positive alternative behaviors. For example, a child may be interested in his father's shop tools but because they are dangerous he must be prevented from playing with them. A behaviorist may recommend that the parent purchase inexpensive toy tools or select a few harmless real tools for the child to play with. Merely punishing the child for playing with his father's tools does not allow for positive alternatives.

While there are many arguments against corporal punishment, nonphysical punishment may also be destructive. For example, Becker (1964) has pointed out that, while love-oriented methods of child rearing and discipline seem, on the surface, to be desirable, it is important to understand that they also involve the withdrawal of love for misbehavior. For some children, the withdrawal of love can be more harmful psychologically than, say, a slap on the hand.

We must not assume that all children are at the same level of emotional or behavioral adjustment. In some rare cases it may be necessary to use corporal contingencies for behavioral control until a child can learn to respond to more positive and humane management approaches. Yet even those who accept that there may be some validity to this line of reasoning usually feel reluctant to advocate corporal punishment, particularly since there are so many viable alternatives available to use.

COMMENT

In the absence of other physical adaptive and protective characteristics, our tendency toward aggression, selfishness, and violence has contributed to our survival in a physically hostile world. Yet, in our contemporary, highly crowded, and technological society, it has become increasingly important that we moderate these aggressive tendencies. There are no more wild frontiers to conquer; we must learn to accommodate ourselves to the limitations of our planet. Our task is to learn how to survive, while maintaining individual and political freedoms.

There is need for progressive intervention at many levels. The physical sciences must develop new technologies that are cleaner, more efficient, and less destructive to the environment. The biological sciences need to learn more about how emotional forces interact with biological phenomena in the development of disease. There is need for broad intervention on the social, political, and economic level that will lead us toward the goal of providing every individual with personal and social freedom, as well as with economic substance. Finally, there must be intervention at the psychological level, intervention that, at the least, may prevent human problems from worsening and, at best, may contribute to individual competence and growth.

Because patterns of self-control are formed in the developing child largely at the interface of youthful desires and environmental limitations, wise management of the disciplinary process would seem to be a fruitful way to foster mature socialization. Perhaps the material we have presented will encourage others to develop richer and broader models of human behavior that will help us increase our knowledge of how to teach ourselves to satisfy our own needs, while respecting the rights of others — so that we may survive in freedom.

REFERENCES

Bandura, A. (1960), Relationship of family patterns to child behavior disorders. Progress Report, U.S.P.H. Research Grant M-1734, Stanford University.

Becker, W. C. (1964), Consequences of different kinds of parental discipline. In: *Review of Child Development Research*, Vol. 1, ed. M. L. Hoffman and L. W. Hoffman. New York: Russell Sage, pp. 169–208.

Ginott, H. G. (1965), *Between Parent and Child*. New York: Macmillan.

———— (1972), *Teacher and Child*. New York: Macmillan.

Subject Index

Name Index

Adler, A., 10, 234
Allen, B. A., xiv, 99–149, 221
Allen, J. G., xiv, 99–149, 221
Allen, J. R., 99, 121, 147
Armstrong, M., 202, 215
Axline, V., 154, 159, 164, 183

Babock, D. E., 149
Baken, D., 5, 12
Bandura, A., 12, 37, 42, 154,
    159, 167, 183, 189, 204, 205,
    214, 215, 252, 253, 255
Barrish, H. H., 203, 215
Baruch, D. W., 152, 154, 183
Baumrind, D., 7, 12
Becker, W. C., 6, 13, 201, 215,
    253, 255
Berne, E., 99, 110, 147
Birch, H. G., 86, 98, 100, 148
Blakeney, R., 148
Bonner, J. W., xii
Brody, M., 98
Brown, M., 148
Brown, R., 47, 61
Bryan, J. H., 58, 62
Burke, K., 49, 62

Campos, L., 148
Cass, L. K., xiii, 15–44, 104, 217,
    218
Chandler, M., xiii, 45–64, 219,
    228
Chess, S., 86, 98, 100, 148
Child, I. I., 26, 44
Church, J., 26, 44

Comenius, J. A., 2, 13
Coopersmith, S., 7, 13, 78, 97

Daly, S., 75, 97
Denneral, D., 98
Deur, J., 4, 13
Dickstein, E., 50, 62
Dobson, J., 4, 13
Dollard, J., 204, 205, 215
Dorr, D., xi, 1–14, 217–255
Dreikurs, R., 10, 13

Ellis, A., 65, 66, 68, 70, 71, 72,
    73, 74, 75, 76, 87, 88, 97, 98,
    111, 220
Erikson, E. H., 10, 13
Ernest, K., 149

Faber, A., 164, 168, 183
Feshback, S., 159, 183
Fraiberg, S., 16, 18, 22, 23, 43,
    44, 152, 183
Freud, A., 18, 23, 43, 44, 154,
    165, 183
Freud, S., 9, 15, 16, 17, 20, 21,
    22, 23, 29, 43
Freyer, M., 7, 14

Gil, D. G., 5, 13, 40, 41, 43, 44
Ginott, H. G., 9, 151–184, 222,
    223, 236, 238, 242–243,
    246–247, 252, 255
Ginsburg, H., 156, 183
Glicken, M. D., 98
Gordon, T., 10, 13, 152, 168, 183

261